Like A Crown

Like A Crown

Adventures in Autism

Robert L. Tucker

authorHOUSE®

AuthorHouse™
1663 Liberty Drive
Bloomington, IN 47403
www.authorhouse.com
Phone: 1-800-839-8640

Published by AuthorHouse   07/26/2012

ISBN: 978-1-4772-2913-2 (sc)
ISBN: 978-1-4772-2912-5 (hc)
ISBN: 978-1-4772-2911-8 (e)

Library of Congress Control Number: 2012911454

"Does It Hang Over My Head Like a Crown?"—Joel Tucker

Dedicated to
my wife Clairissa
for her constant and loving support
of Joel Tucker

Contents

Introduction

This book is primarily a book about Joel Arlitt Tucker, autistic since birth. He is not considered high-functionally autistic, at least not to the point of having Asperger's Syndrome, but neither is he low-functionally autistic. He displays most, but not all, of the traits typical of autism. Like all people (okay, most), he is fascinating and worth getting to know. But this book is not intended to be simply about Joel, but, rather, it is designed as a help manual for parents, teachers, and all people who are involved in helping autistic people. As you read, substitute the name of Joel for any autistic child or adult you know.

It is hoped that this book will provide tools and techniques which will aid in the understanding of autism and will communicate to society at large the needs, problems, and joys of autistic people. While it is expected that much of the information contained herein is useful, much of it is also philosophical and perhaps even esoteric at times. Like a cafeteria or a mosaic with lots of variety, not all of this book will be beneficial or apropos to every individual with autism disability. Yet, there is no question that, regardless of your level of contact with autism, you will find yourself engaging with an autistic person at some point in your life. Maybe the information herein can be called upon in those instances.

Sometimes it is difficult, maybe even impossible, to be entirely objective toward your own child, and there is little doubt that the subsequent pages will display some bias on our part concerning our son. Yet I have attempted to share the frustrations along with the joys, the confusions and the solutions, the fear and the courage, the humor with the serious, and the anger with the compassion. An entire range of emotions is displayed when dealing with autism, and, for us, the vast array of emotions has been manifest throughout Joel's life. In the end, however, it is our love for our son that has held us together and our love that sustains us throughout his life.

This is not an ordinary "How-To" book with any kind of step-by-step progression of dealing with autistic children. Rather, this is a collection of stories, challenges, joys, and fears that have accompanied our efforts to give Joel the best environment we could provide. In these pages, readers will gain knowledge of autism, of parenting, and they will hopefully smile a time or two. Readers may also learn what not to do and things to avoid. For parents of autistic children, this book is intended as a comfort to know that all your efforts are worthwhile; nothing is in vain. For the outside world, this book may be revealing and might remind all "normal" people that there are autistics and that they deserve an opportunity to be successful. For educators, this book will serve partly as a manual for dealing with those children who are labeled "autistic". Although autism is broad-spectrum, meaning that it is not necessarily a specific problem, remember that it does not, in its basic definition, affect natural intelligence. A person can be very intelligent with autism or have many learning disabilities with autism. It is a myth that autism means the person is brilliant but "trapped". This myth is caused by the movies and stories of special gifts. Your autistic child may or may not have special gifts. Being autistic guarantees nothing.

Organized in a way to keep the pages turning, each chapter has a different approach and tone. While the chapters can be read independently, the book is most engaging when read beginning to end. It is not a chronological study of Joel's life and does not following "growing up" order. Rather, the book deals with stories and concepts intended to aid parents, teachers, and community leaders with any autistic children or adults they encounter. One additional note, the word 'NORMAL' is a terribly nebulous word used mostly in opposition to disabled. Since 'normal' cannot be defined, and who, after all, is truly normal, it will be used sparingly. When it is used, it refers to a person who is not autistic or who is not disabled. The term 'Special Needs' is also used occasionally, instead of autism, as a way to imply the provisions required for meeting the needs of the disabled.

When we learn how autistic people react to outward stimuli, we discover the reasons for their actions, how they learn, and how they communicate, and we ultimately learn about ourselves, thereby making the world a more congenial environment for everyone. There is much to learn. Let the journey begin . . .

One

He is Autistic

Autism is a neurological disorder that encompasses a broad spectrum of learning disabilities, including, but not limited to, Asperger's Syndrome and several developmentally delayed characteristics. Autism is not a behavioral disorder.

On December 8, 1989, Joel Arlitt Tucker was born at approximately 6:30 P.M. His Apgar scores were high, signifying a healthy baby. It was a forceps vaginal delivery resulting in Joel having a bruised nose and a broken collarbone. Joel's brother, Jacob, who had been a caesarian baby, was anxiously looking forward to meeting his new brother. Jacob was three years old when Joel was born.

While Jacob's development matched the textbook presentations, in some ways he was advanced. His language skills were quite precocious, and he demonstrated a strong and determined countenance, a high level of curiosity, exceptional intelligence, and, mostly, a great deal of care and compassion. These qualities remain true today. Among the sad things of Joel's disabilities was the realization that Joel would not become the sports partner Jacob was seeking.

After Joel came home, he seemed like a normal infant. Having been down this road before with Jacob, we were a little more confident with our parenting of infants. Joel, in fact, seemed to catch on more quickly to breastfeeding than did Jacob. With a healthy appetite, Joel's bodily functions were normal, and he responded in textbook fashion during the first few months.

We became aware of some delays at approximately six months when he had trouble sitting up for any period of time and did not become mobile until several months later. Careful reading, however, reminded us that some infants are slower than others at crawling. He did seem excessively quiet at times, and quite calm, overall.

With Joel vocalizing less than Jacob had, we attributed it to Jacob's precociousness and his unusual desire to succeed. It was because of Joel's lack of being able to walk and become potty-trained that we first began to accept the possibility of some developmental delays. Plus, his frequent ear infections seemed to contribute to many of his problems, and we attributed his delays to being a sickly child.

Relocating from Louisiana to Texas when Joel was approximately one year old, we rationalized his problems as being the trauma of moving along with the excessive ear infections. Getting ear tubes at age three, we hoped that it would cure the slow language development and inattention to the seemingly obvious. By the time we were definitely aware of a problem, we had already fallen into the pattern of constantly worrying about Joel and always looking out for him.

As do all parents of disabled children, we sought a cure, some kind of fix-it-fast system that would make our son normal, perhaps like his older brother. But in order to find the answers, we needed to know what was wrong. Hearing about a diagnostic camp where Joel would be tested for physical and mental impairments, we began to make plans for his extended stay.

The camp was located outside of Gonzales, Texas and included room, board, and comprehensive testing for children. At no cost to us, this camp, sponsored by the Elks Lodge, has provided many years of service to disabled children and their parents.

The three weeks without Joel were difficult, but we made the sacrifice in the hopes of getting answers about his future. He was four years old at the time. The marvelous camp came to an end, and with it we had several pages of diagnostic results and suggestions for his future. The term 'Pervasive Developmental Disorder' was used frequently in the report, a term we did not fully understand but did accept. Pervasive Developmental Disorder is generally the label ascribed to a child who may or may not later be considered autistic. It is the first step toward a diagnosis. Included in the report were various other items, such as a shortage of mercury, a shortage of certain enzymes, a possible aversion to both gluten and casein, and several physical challenges.

It was beneficial but did not meet our expectations in many ways. We wanted a cure, but instead we received the news that Joel was delayed. We now had a term to match his problems, but no obvious fix-it solution. But in many ways, it was nice to say to people and to his school that he was developmentally delayed due to having Pervasive Developmental Disorder.

The word 'autism' was being batted about in our minds, but we were not yet comfortable with the term. Keep in mind that the term 'autism' was undergoing a transformation of sorts during the 1980s and 1990s. What was once considered a result of poor parenting, or, more specifically, a "refrigerator mother", was now being recognized as a neurological weakness with heredity being of greater cause than environment. While it is a little disconcerting to parents to believe that something from the past in the DNA, or in the family might have caused the problem, it is certainly a more acceptable reason than poor parenting to accept. It is easier and more accurate to blame our great-great grandfather than Mom!

We may have intuitively known that Joel was autistic, but it took time to accept the diagnosis. One other challenge associated with autism is the awareness that there is no cure. When parents learn that their child is autistic, it feels synonymous to no hope for the future—certainly an unacceptable position for any parent. Autism feels like a kick in the teeth to a parent, and nobody wants such a feeling. Connected to this was Joel's dislike of the term 'autistic', which is true today. He prefers the term 'disabled' and often refers to himself as a disabled adult.

Meanwhile, we tried to exist as a normal family of five. The birth of Jordan was yet another blessing, and although small at birth, Jordan quickly displayed the same precocious signs of his oldest brother. He was quick to learn, highly energetic, curious, and seemed ready to conquer the next task. A delightful child, Jordan's incredible creativity surpassed that of the rest of his family, and even today he remains a creatively gifted young man.

Joel was diagnosed as having Autism Spectrum Disorder when he was five years old. A battery of tests administered through the school system determined what we, in fact, already knew; he was autistic. We may have harbored a hope that he would be considered as having Asperger's Syndrome, but his verbal skills were not advanced enough for this diagnosis. Asperger's Syndrome is generally considered a form of autism but is characterized by high-functioning skills and higher performance on IQ tests. Often, children with this diagnosis are quick to learn but display social retardation more than cognitive or physical limitations.

Having Joel labeled 'autistic' was both liberating and frightening to us, but it did allow Joel to receive a little more needed attention and some modifications for his education. While we did not, in any sense, celebrate his disability, it was also comforting to know what the problem was and what to expect.

It also made us realize that our family did not match the typical American family very well. When other families would go out to eat, go to the mall, or go over to someone's house, and the normal parental concerns would take place concerning their children, for us it was a level of fear and concern not experienced by others. Yes, we worried about his safety, particularly since he did not seem to have any instincts about danger or the potential for injury. But nearly equal to this was his propensity to do something embarrassing and inappropriate, such as flicking the lights on and off, pulling out tissues and leaving them on the floor, wandering around the house, getting into closets, crawling under beds, running, standing in front of the television set, and constantly demanding food or drink.

These behaviors were common for Joel but caused us great hesitation in social settings. We found ourselves resistant to friendship gatherings, social situations, concerts, and even going out to eat. We became a closer family by virtue of our isolation, an isolation born out of the protection of both our reputation as parents and for the safety of Joel.

Joel was a lovable child, but his unpredictable and often disruptive behavior often caused great resentment and anger in others. Many were the times when we would receive pointed "suggestions" for improvement of Joel with veiled parenting ideas for us.

In fact, those early years with Joel reminded me of all the times I had quickly criticized parents for the behavior of their children. In my early arrogance, I was convinced that parents needed to be firmer with children, except in those cases where I thought the parent was being overly harsh and creating rebellion rather than subduing it. I had all the answers back then.

One criticism does remain, however, and that is when the parent keeps the behavior in the public limelight. A crying child in a concert is excessively disturbing, and a screaming fit in a mall is quite distracting. These kinds of behaviors ought to be kept away from other people whenever possible. Knowing that, we preferred to keep Joel away from the public eye. It was simply easier not to have to deal with the stares, the criticism, the curiosity, and the judgments.

Historically, parents would usually give children with learning problems to an institution, and, going back hundreds of years, those children would be placed in some kind of asylum where they would usually decline. In other words, parents and society would collectively give up on the children, relegating them to an unfulfilled life and an early death. This is not necessarily a diatribe against the earlier practice of institutionalization, a practice that is still necessary in certain instances. In fact, many parents believed that "an expert" or that skilled caregivers would be more helpful than having the child stay at home. As difficult as it may be to admit, we wrestled with this idea at times ourselves, quickly rejecting it, though, with a degree of optimism about Joel's future.

We hear discussions about the quality of life, about contributing citizens, about the role of education, and about helping people become productive in the world. We have great respect for those figures, who, through grit, fortitude, and intelligence, accomplish amazing feats and become icons of the American Dream. We come across headlines and smile when we read about a sports figure, an actor, a model, or a popular musician who has achieved notoriety. We hold these people in high esteem. But we also regard with deserved admiration the brain surgeon, the lawyer, the politician, the general, and the successful businessman, all of whom contribute brilliance and skills to the betterment of society.

My other two children are of this ilk. One is on the path to becoming a sports psychologist. He is strong, smart, driven to excellence, and will not allow himself to fail at what he does. The other son is creative, gifted, and bright, with a broad sense of the musical world, a world he is ready to enter and to conquer.

But what about those children and those adults who do not have the ability to become famous actors, lawyers, doctors, teachers, or athletes? Do they have a role in society? Do they deserve a chance to live, to progress, to fulfill their potential? Does the government have a responsibility to help these people? Where does the family fit in with this obligation? Should we practice some kind of Teutonic eugenics that is an extension of Darwinism and let these people strike out on their own? Would the inevitable failure teach them how to succeed? Or would the inevitable failure result in more homeless people dying in the streets?

Whether you are a believer in God or not, can you honestly embrace the principal of the survival of the fittest and sit back and allow those with special needs to suffer? Should we, as contributing citizens of the world, shrug our shoulders and let these special-needs people enter the world only to live in sorrow and confusion? The bird with the broken wing will likely perish due to its inability to sustain itself. Maybe a few injured birds will figure out how to live, but most will not. This is the way of the world. Let things happen the way they happen—correct?

But let's look at this another way. Through no fault of their own, autistics are born into a world that in many ways remains a mystery to them throughout their lives. They have a right to live in this world and a right to make their own way. Those without special needs (although I could argue that everyone has special needs) often feel that they have a moral obligation to help those who are challenged to adjust to the complex world.

It seems to me that we have one of two choices with these people: 1) give up or 2) help them. Since choice number one is not a choice in the Tucker family, we have elected to help our son, Joel, cope in a difficult world that does not and cannot fully understand his disabilities. Some may call this 'family love'; others may call this 'moral obligation', but whatever it is called, it is the unswerving, relentless quest to help our son and to provide for his safety, comfort, and security.

Our attitude would not let us give up on Joel, and we certainly never made any serious plans for an institution. For one thing, he was and still is intelligent. He displays prowess in particular areas

11

and continues to surprise us with his perception and awareness of the world. He can learn, and he has improved immensely over the years, both in his behavior and in his ability to cope. From the beginning up to the present time, we have focused on Joel's successes, minor though they may appear to the outside world.

He is constantly rewarded for looking nice, and he is generally rewarded for good behavior. He is praised when he talks, when he is nice, when he picks up after himself, when he eats properly with good manners, when he acts appropriately, and anytime he does the right thing. We never miss an opportunity to be positive with him, but we are also not afraid to remind him of the need to improve. When he does something inappropriate or socially unacceptable, we are quick to correct him and point out the correct behavior. Picking his nose is one of those actions that will bring quick correction and a reminder to get a tissue.

Dealing with Joel's obsessions and compulsions has been difficult, comedic, bewildering, aggravating, and vastly entertaining at times. Requiring nonstop energy to keep up with the latest problem, we have dedicated ourselves to his happiness and satisfaction about things that really do not matter that much. In most families, there is an old truism that when Mama is happy, everyone's happy. In our case that is true, but nearly equal is the truism that when Joel is happy, everyone's happy. Joel's times of unhappiness are so trying that nobody wants to relive the experience.

Throughout our lives, we have often walked on "eggshells" to avoid the anger fit, the frustration, or the insistence on certain things. It has often been easier simply to give in than to go to battle with Joel's problem. This has made our family life one of Joel's life. To do otherwise was to inflict great emotional stress on everyone.

This is not to say that Jacob and Jordan have never received attention. In fact, I have suspected that their successes and their drive to excellence has been generated partly due to the ongoing challenges of Joel, almost making up for what Joel lacks.

In Jacob's room and in Jordan's room are trophies, medals, certificates, plaques, and ribbons demonstrating their athletic successes, music awards, academics, and social engagements, all of which we are proud and none we would want to take away. But in Joel's room is a marked lack of the same external rewards.

Oh, there are a few things, like the Howdy Doody award and the various spelling awards, both of which have great meaning to Joel—and should. But they do not represent great effort as much as aptitude and attitude. Joel's spelling prowess is born out of an early interest in the alphabet and how words are formed. While it is certainly a gift, it is not necessarily something that was educated, but, in fact, came naturally to him. Unfortunately, his ability to spell does not lead to greater comprehension, but rather only to word construction accuracy.

The Howdy Doody award seems rather trite on the surface. He got the award due to coming into school every day with a big smile and a desire to say hello to everyone. But, in fact, the award demonstrates what is possibly Joel's greatest strength—to make others feel good. This gift is one that cannot be diminished and one that will likely remain true throughout his life. It is what gives his life greater meaning and often is the very trait we return to when we think about his future. Joel harbors no ill will toward anyone, and he has a natural compassion and forgiveness that he wears on his sleeve everywhere he goes. His appearance is snappy and is usually accompanied by a dress shirt and a tie. He almost has an obsession with ties (He has always enjoyed something around his neck.) and owns a sizable collection of ties of all types. His sharp look is often deceiving, giving him the persona of a successful businessman or banker.

Joel's endearing charm is also his potential harm. The knowledge of good and evil is, unfortunately, our blessing and curse in life.

Knowing about evil is often something we wish we did not have, but, in truth, our knowledge protects us from danger. Joel does not have discernment in determining evil or danger. To him, all is well; all people are good; all situations are positive, and everyone and everything is to be embraced. Like an innocent puppy or a child, Joel requires us to watch out for him. While we wish him to retain his optimistic expectations, at the same time, we also provide a hedge of protection to be placed around him most of the time.

We are his legal guardians, and the angels have helped us out a time or two! We try to make sure they are not working overtime, though, and much of our time is spent watching out for Joel but also teaching him as much independence as he is capable of handling. We have not wished to smother him with a security blanket, but we also have a responsibility to look out for him. Somewhere there is a balance. It is the same balance all parents seek—to love and protect our children while allowing them freedom to be who they wish to be, to succeed on their own, to learn from their mistakes, to forge their own paths, and to realize their potential. Regardless of Joel's limitations and our obligation to keep him free from danger, we also continue to allow him, at least to a certain extent, the opportunity to succeed and to grow from the challenges presented.

Two

Playing The Cards
You Have Been Dealt

One morning I pulled into the Starbucks coffee shop, when two friends showed up and asked how I was doing. We visited for a minute, and I asked about one of their family members who had been having some personal problems. We talked about that for a minute, and I expressed my sadness for this person and my wish that all would turn out for the best. One of these friends shrugged and said, "You play the cards that life has dealt to you."

While this philosophy is not exactly new, or even very deep, it does contain truth on several levels. I am not a poker player or much of a card player. I have never played Bridge or Canasta, and I am only superficially knowledgeable in the game of Spades. Although I am not judgmental about cards, or even poker, and I am glad that people gain pleasure and emotional satisfaction from their card-playing experiences, I am suspicious of addictive behavior, which, in turn, makes me question gambling as a source of entertainment, but that is a subject for another day. I do assume that the expression of "playing the cards you have been dealt," grew out of some old cowboy kind of practice from the Old West. As an aside, many great life philosophies did come out of the Old West, including, "watch your back," and, "keep your horse tied up." The idea of playing the cards you have been dealt obviously means that you may not have picked these particular cards, but you still have to do the best you can with them no matter what.

Life is like that . . . to an extent. We don't always get to choose the events that happen to us. While we often create our own problems or our own happiness, and we do get opportunities to make choices, there are times when things just simply happen. The events that happen may not be our choice, but how we react to those events can make a difference in subsequent events.

We have an autistic son. We did not choose to have an autistic son, and we did not intend for that to happen. His presence in our lives is a joy, but it is also a challenge. My point is that not only do we need to do our best to help Joel, but we also need to recognize that Joel is not just a difficult card to play but, in fact, is an ace! Of course—people are not cards, and life is not just a game, but it is true that we should take what we have been given and turn it into a positive.

Blessings come in many different forms, and we must constantly reflect upon those blessings. What may seem like an unfair card to you might, in fact, be the card that provides significance for you at a later date. It has been said that when a door closes, a window opens, and that opportunity may seem disguised but is often right in front of us.

You probably did not choose all of the events that have happened to you, but you had a choice in how you dealt with those events. Too often, we expend emotional energy to whine about our problems instead of applying energy in finding solutions. Take the events that occur, react with dignity, and reach for positive results.

Now that I have postured a philosophy of, "playing the cards you have been given," and playing them well, it is time for me to practice what I write. Best wishes as you play the game of life today. Use your cards to help someone. Use them well and wisely.

Three

The Wreck

It was a warm Saturday afternoon, and I was in the living room reading and waiting for the dryer to stop, while my wife was in the kitchen, planning supper. The baby was asleep. Jacob was playing with Legos, and our four-year-old son Joel was driving my truck and getting in a wreck. Yes, that's right. We had seen Joel a few minutes earlier while he was walking through the house. The garage door leading from the laundry room to the garage was open, and my wife asked me rather casually where my black truck was parked. I told her that it was in the garage where it always was, but she responded with, "You must have parked it somewhere else, since it is not there." This was followed by us both asking in unison, "Where's Joel?"

At that point, we heard a car horn, and we both ran from the kitchen, through the laundry room, into the garage, and outside, where we saw my black truck with the emergency lights flashing. It was across the street, facing our house, with the back bumper smashed against a parked car. On either side of my truck, there were cars that had stopped to see the wreck and find out why a truck was perpendicular to the street and blocking traffic.

In the driver's seat, and looking very happy, was our four-year-old autistic boy with his hands on the steering wheel. Apparently, he had crawled into the truck, released the parking brake, turned on the emergency lights, rolled backward out of the garage, down the driveway, across the street, and ended up against a parked car.

After settling down the people who were getting out of their vehicles, convincing one lady that I was not the worst father on the planet, and then routing traffic around the truck, I proceeded to promise the owner of the car, who came out of his house after hearing the ruckus, that we would pay for the repairs. Meanwhile, my wife carried Joel back into our house, while I returned the truck to the garage. Things soon began to settle down once again.

The car repair was $300 . . . along with several apologies. Also, we began closing the garage door more often. In retrospect, we have wondered about several things concerning that incident—How did Joel pull it off? How did he escape injury? How did he get out of our sight that quickly?

Joel's lack of social awareness and his unique approach to the world in which we live give him his own personal goals, which are different from those of most people. His world is a special world and a beautiful world—a world without danger, without suspicion, and without fear. Unfortunately, the real world is a scary place. Yet for all the potential challenges, Joel is a lucky boy! The angels around him work hard, but it is always worth it.

Four

Character Trait: Lack of Prejudice

We normally think of prejudice as pre-judging a person based on skin color, but prejudice can actually assume many forms.

I came out of the grocery store, pushing a cart and walking beside my son, Joel. As I walked toward my pickup, I saw two boys and felt a stirring of suspicion and even dislike within me. The boys were covered in tattoos, had spiked hair, had body piercings in strange places, and one was smoking a cigarette. I was disgusted with their appearance, turned away quickly, and wondered why they weren't in jail yet. With that thought came the rampant metaphors and analogies of cancers, sores, blights, cuts, bruises, bacteria, and many other maladies that these boys inflicted on our society. The world would be better off without such sub-humans walking around.

But, not for the first time and certainly not the last, Joel taught me a lesson. As I neared my truck, I heard, "Hey, Joel, how's it going?" I looked around and saw those two sub-humans smiling and shaking Joel's hand. He smiled back and began talking to them. Apparently, he knew them from school from a couple of years earlier. Had they changed their demeanor upon seeing Joel, knowing his innocence and charm? Or, in fact, was their appearance deliberately misleading and Joel could see through it?

As I watched this scene unfold, I realized several things.

One: my autistic son had once again offered his magic to the world and made it a better place. He has an unusual ability to share unadulterated joy with others. He brings no prejudice with him, no suspicion, no fear, and no judgment to the table. He offers up care, interest, and acceptance to all people, regardless of their status, appearance, age, background, race, beliefs, world-view, and position. He does not need, nor does he desire, to correct anyone, criticize anyone, give his opinions on anything, or pass judgment in any way. He simply wants to say hello, to be friendly, and make the world a better place. He gives the gift of simplicity and love to everyone he meets. He is the season of Christmas every day of the year (Of course, he has had those occasional but pointed times of being a sixteen year old, but I don't want to talk about that right now since it ruins the lesson I learned!).

Two: My attitude was prejudiced. I had pre-judged the two boys based on their appearance, and I made decisions that were decidedly unfair. I had assumed that tattoos, body piercings, and a cigarette meant those boys had criminal intent. I labeled them without knowing them. I rejected them while having no foundation for my attitude. Now this is not to say that I completely agree with their appearance choices. I wish, for their sake, that they would consider another avenue for their expression of independence. Although I was wrong to pre-judge them, I do suspect that finding employment has been a challenge for these two. But as far as their character, work ethic, compassion, integrity, and personality—none of these things have been determined. Certainly their appearance is not enough to decide these other qualities.

Three: You never know who your friends or your family members may know. It pays to be friendly to all.

I will work diligently to avoid future prejudices, and, instead, I will offer up the kind of automatic acceptance which Joel is able to give. If the world had more people like Joel, it would be a better place.

Five

The Missing Boy

Where's Joel? This was the three-minute question, especially when he was three years old. When Joel first began to walk, and up until recently, as well as sometimes now, we began to ask every three minutes, "Where's Joel?" But even with the three-minute check, we lost him a few times. One of the first times occurred right after he had turned three years old: My wife was in the kitchen; I was in the bedroom, and Joel was in his room . . . or was he? I heard the proverbial, "Where's Joel?" and answered, "In his room!" A few minutes later, she asked again, followed by, "Are you sure?" I said, "Yes," but with a question in my tone. I quickly walked to his room and realized that he was gone. We covered the house in a short time but could not find him anywhere. While the back door was locked, the front door was open, so we tore out the front door while she went left and I went right. Several houses down the street, I found some of my wife's shoes on the sidewalk. I ran quicker and saw an older teenager holding Joel. Assuming the worst, I ran breathlessly to the boy who had a big smile on his face and was bringing Joel back. He told us that he had seen Joel crossing the street and recognized him as ours. Once again, the angels surrounding Joel had to work overtime . . . but they did their job.

Once we got over the incident, and I promised that I would actually check on Joel rather than assume he was still where he was three minutes earlier, we found ourselves laughing as we imagined him in his underclothes walking down the street in ladies shoes.

The "Where's Joel?" practice did not help one Saturday when we went to Six Flags in Arlington, Texas. As we exited a ride, Joel twisted out of my grasp, got separated from us, and took off running in the opposite direction from which we were going. Within a few seconds, he was lost in the crowd of thousands and completely out of our sight. We took off running in his direction but could not seem to get through the crowd, plus, we had two other boys to keep close to us. I told my wife to watch the boys and that I would get Joel. As I yelled, "Excuse me," and looked frantically for Joel, I heard above the crowd, "We have Joel; don't worry." As I got closer to the voice and saw Joel's face above the people, I saw some acquaintances from church who happened to be at Six Flags that same day. They had recognized Joel, grabbed him for us, and held him high above the crowd for me to see.

Angels take on many shapes and sizes, from friends, to acquaintances, and neighbors. While not everyone out there is good, the good ones are in abundance and make the world a better place. To those people and countless others, I say, "Thank you."

Six

Finding His Potential

As I sit on my front porch, looking out on the dead grass and wondering when it will rain, it occurs to me that even a little water could and would promote green growth in the grass. All I have to do is get out the hose and water the grass. The grass has potential, but I need to help it. I choose, however, not to water the grass, due to the expense and the time needed. So the grass withers away, turns brown, and becomes totally dependent upon nature for its sustenance.

While I recognize the potential in the grass for improvement, I do nothing about it. I give up on it and elect to spend my time and energy on other things . . . after all . . . it is just grass. But people are different. We should value people as individuals, and there is no excuse for giving up on anyone. Of course, there are times when we have to let people go their own way and make their own decisions, but there are other times when direct action is required. Such is the case with Joel, our autistic son.

When Joel was a child, he was late at sitting up, walking, toilet training, talking, and virtually everything else that our oldest son did "right on time". As an autistic child, Joel's potential is not in the usual successes the world deems as important. A world that prizes academic achievements, athletic prowess, making money, traveling, promotions, and public success, has a difficult time embracing a person of Joel's disability. What is his potential, and how can Joel succeed? In what areas can Joel excel?

What Joel does excel in is making other people smile and providing joy in their lives. His potential may not include playing football, saving lives as a doctor, developing a new invention, or entertaining thousands, but how many of us can actually claim to transform a room with openness and instant acceptance? While most of us remain busy accomplishing and meeting our goals, while trying to make a difference in the world in some dynamic and real way, it is Joel who does the most by virtue of his gifts.

When asked who his best friend is, he always answers, "Everyone!" He loves everyone, and those who take the time to know him love him back.

We will never give up on Joel. We will always see his potential and help him reach as high as he can. While his "highest" may not be the same definition as other people's definition, in many ways, Joel's accomplishments may, in fact, be greater than most. We continue to provide a loving, warm, firm, disciplined, but compassionate environment for Joel, and, mostly, we continue to see the potential for and in Joel. While autism itself is incurable, it is educable. Nurturing, guiding, and helping are, for Joel, the water that helps him grow.

Although the difficult times (and there have been many of those) give us a moment's pause, we continue to move forward with the "water" without regard of the time, energy, and expense. I often remind my boys not to be more trouble than they are worth. The truth is, they and all children are always worth the trouble!

One of the hardest things about parenting an autistic child is to keep high expectations as part of the behavioral standard while recognizing the reality and the limitations. Unfortunately, there is no magic formula or secret recipe for this kind of balance. It is a process of constantly keeping the ideal in mind but also remaining aware of the reality of what it means to be autistic.

An autistic child has limitations—many of them. Their world is not like ours, and they simply cannot do the things other people can do. Life moves too quickly for them and often appears random and without the required order. There is usually an abundance of stimulation, noise, complexity, color, and confusions surrounding our lives, and an autistic tends to shut down amidst the chaos. In addition, the lack of physical coordination contributes to a sluggish and awkward existence, making crossing streets, reaching for things, writing, and general mobility rather difficult. Usually not being able to drive and almost not able to navigate public transportation, they are reliant on help to accomplish any task not readily accessible. Computers are potentially liberating in many ways, but for an autistic, a computer is simply another machine full of complex problems and over-stimulation.

More limitations are caused by a lack of curiosity, little imagination, few dreams, and the inability to use any creativity in solving problems. All these and more are debilitating realities of the life of an autistic. Ironically and comfortingly, at least to an extent, they do not always recognize their own limits, but, instead, they learn how to cope and how to exist successfully within their small framework of ability.

But, as I told Joel, he cannot use his disabilities as an excuse for mediocrity or poor behavior. To this end, we have invoked a list of required high expectations and goals for our son, and we constantly encourage him to reach for these requirements. Some are rather trivial in some ways, involving hygiene, life-skills, and coping techniques, while other requirements are substantial and complicated. Each day we remind him of his goals, and each day we present several high expectations to him. Obviously, if the goals are unattainable, we risk disappointment, depression, and stress. On the other hand, if the goals are too simple, then he has nothing for which to strive.

This all creates a healthy balance of respecting the reality of the situation without letting go of the ideal. This is necessary in the parenting of a disabled child, and we have done that for twenty years with some degree of both success and failure. My wife and I often ask ourselves, "What can he accomplish?" or, "What is the best thing for Joel?" These questions and more govern our actions as guardians and dictate our goals for him. Without being imperialistic, however, we also encourage Joel to set his own goals and to reach for the highest in all things. This is particularly important as his adult years set in.

Joel's own goals are usually immediate and involve some sort of gratification of the senses. His lack of a concept of time prevents him from forecasting or projecting the future. This means that we encourage him to develop his short-term goals, but we guide him toward the longer term, always remaining committed to the balance of high expectations and a recognition of reality.

As I write this chapter, I am reminded that, though his limitations are different from those of other people, and though the dreams may be framed by his autism, the process for helping Joel is not dissimilar to helping anyone . . . including ourselves. We should dream big and relentlessly pursue the ideal, but we should also be shaped by our current reality. It all makes for a wonderfully complex culture and one that is guaranteed to keep us hopping.

Seven

Hope and Acceptance

Each morning, after we knew something was wrong and after we had done some preliminary research into the problem, we often prayed that something magical and wonderful had occurred during the night. Maybe the 'normal' fairy had visited Joel and waved a wand containing 'typical' and 'common' dust all over him, and that he would awaken as the same Joel but with only the normal characteristics found in young boys his age.

Each morning we would wake him, full of hope and desire that all the problems would have disappeared into the night and that Joel would be all the things we wanted him to be. But all our hopes were in vain. Instead, day after day, we encountered the same autistic boy he was the day before—no change, no hope—and no altering of the truth. Our Joel was, and is, autistic.

The days turned into weeks, the weeks into months, and the months into years. We eventually accepted that there was no magic cure and no sudden change, that Joel would not suddenly become the boy we wanted him to be. The passing of time resulted in a type of resignation of reality, an acceptance of the truth and no longer a fatuous belief in the dream of the transformation of our son.

But as the years melded together, we began *our* transformation. I am not sure if the change happened suddenly or if it was a slow but deliberate altering of our unconscious preconceptions. Our acceptance and resignation of who Joel actually was became something new and exciting. We changed, and, with that, we changed our view of Joel. Instead of being an anomaly with limited gifts and peculiar behavior, Joel became a superb example of all that is good in human nature.

While previously on each day we had sought changes in Joel, instead, what we ultimately sought was change in ourselves. It was our hearts that transformed and our minds that changed and our goals that found the truth. Instead of imagining the golden horizon of perfection that existed in our dreams, our dreams were and are right in front of us. The golden utopia and the amalgamation of our hearts and minds are manifest in Joel, our son. It is Joel who makes the world a better place; it is Joel who offers love, patience, tolerance, and, above all, joy . . . to everyone he meets.

Now, on each day, we awaken, anxiously anticipating the boy who has made a difference in all of us. The magic dust that we looked for happened many years ago; it happened to Joel, to us, and it also happens to those who meet him. Your happiness may be in front of you. Find it; embrace it, and be thankful for it. Joy comes in many forms and many sizes . . . for us, it is our children, and we love Joel just the way he is. We now recognize the blessing poured upon us in the form of this incredible boy—Joel. We did not deserve him, but he is ours just the same. For that we are lucky and thankful.

Eight

Medication Mistakes

Medicating Joel has been an experimental and learning process that has evolved through many mistakes and some successes up to the present time. As parents who were desperate to find an answer or at least some sort of medical help for Joel, we searched through journals, magazines, and sought a myriad of physicians' opinions. To deal with his allergies, Joel was taken through difficult and painful allergy tests, and for over a year he was injected with various anti-allergy medications.

In addition, Joel was medicated for ear problems, sleep problems, bladder-control problems, behavioral problems, learning problems, and physiological problems. We have worked through homeopathy, vitamins, enzymes, minerals, and many types of behavioral improvement drugs. Each new regime invited a hope of improvement, a false sense of optimism, and finally a big disappointment.

I recall using a common drug for many years when we continued to increase his dosage to insure proper behavior for his obvious hyperactivity and Attention Deficit Disorder. After steadily adding more of the drug to his body, I one day realized how thin he had become and how extreme was his behavior. I took him off the drug (only to be fussed at for improperly dealing with my son by a physician in another city) and watched him gain fifteen pounds in a few weeks.

One time, we made an appointment with a so-called specialist who came highly recommended. We subsequently spent $250, plus a motel room fee, only to have the specialist see him for a total of fifteen minutes and inform us that he was very slow to obey. He wrote a prescription for yet another different but similar behavior-altering medication. Within three weeks, we recognized that he once again was losing weight and was rebounding dramatically more hyper from the medicine each evening. We decided not to return to that physician, but we forgot to cancel the next appointment and received a "no-show" bill for $150!

Many years and many medications later, we did our own exhaustive research and discovered a correlation between various neurological disorders and autism. Autism is primarily a neurological problem—not a behavioral one. Although the cause of autism continues to be debated, ultimately, it is a weakness in the brain neurology that results in a wide disparity of problems within the autism spectrum. Following this conclusion, we conferred with a physician who agreed to try but would also monitor a drug to treat the neurological problem rather than the behavioral one. The medication we now use regularly is one type used for schizophrenia. This does not mean that autism is a form of schizophrenia or that the two disabilities are even related, but it does serve as a reminder that autism is primarily neurological. With this idea in mind, we continue to hope for the day that scientists and DNA mathematicians identify the weakness in the DNA, thereby leading to a cure.

We immediately noticed vast improvement and continue to be thrilled with the results, although things are far from perfect. While we do not reject the power of vitamins and behavior modification techniques, we are happy right now with our medication choice. It is quite expensive, and we continue to search for the correct insurance package that will adequately meet our needs.

But amidst our journey for Joel, truth emerged. Ultimately we realized, in our constant quest for the right medication for our son, that we had actually discovered the secret ingredient to success for Joel. It was right in front of our noses for years and was the same ingredient we used for our other children. We had applied a constant and devoted emotion to Joel that we use today; it is called "unconditional love" and will never change.

Nine

Literal expressions

While driving to another city one night and needing to make a stop, we looked for the best place that would be quick but provide some necessities. After stopping the truck and getting out in the coldest part of winter, I said, "Brrr . . . it's colder than a banker's heart out here," and we proceeded to hurry into the store. We bought a couple of things, got back in the truck, and headed out.

Approximately thirty minutes later, from the back seat, I heard Joel, age twenty, say, "Dad, why do you say colder than a banker's heart? Why don't you say colder than a polar bear's heart, or a teacher's heart, or a worker's heart, or anything else? Why do you say banker?"

Joel's disability causes a lack of understanding of subtleties, expressions, and clichés, particularly those kinds of phrases that are metaphorical or analogous. This problem is connected to the lack of creativity which is inherent with forms of autism, a missing element that allows for a depth of thinking and a perception of the environment. Unfortunately, creativity can also be the element that leads to deception, lying, stealing, and manipulation—all traits that do not exist in Joel.

An expression such as, "cold as a banker's heart," not only compares weather conditions to a person, but it also compares the situation to a particular item, in this case—a heart. In addition, it requires a depth of concept of the heart that goes beyond the physical thing and into an emotional analysis. So a person who hears this phrase processes it in several ways: 1) It is cold outside, 2) A banker is a person who works in a bank, 3) A heart keeps the blood flowing in the body, 4) A heart is also used as a reference tool for love and compassion in a person, 5) A cold heart is not literally possible without death, 6) In this case, the heart is an emotion, and 7) The emotion must be a lack of compassion. After putting these things together, the typical person might smile (If he is a banker, he might be irritated!), might disagree, might laugh uproariously (doubtful), or simply focus attention on the cold weather rather than considering the insult to the poor and innocent (Is that possible?) banker!

Back to Joel. When he heard this phrase, he was not able to process through the phrase and conclude both that it is cold and a banker is without compassion. In fact, the phrase makes no literal sense whatsoever. No person living can have a cold heart. A banker is a living person. He does not have a cold heart; therefore, the phrase is not a truth.

But the phrase also has another problem for Joel. It assumes that people are aware of the bias against banking officers who call in debts and are without the attribute of forgiveness. Yet, for Joel, there are two problems: 1) He does not have an understanding of the role of a banker, 2) He does not understand insults or the negative actions of people. Joel believes in the good in everyone and has never met anyone he doesn't like. In fact, Joel cannot imagine a person doing anything bad to another person. Everyone is good, so how can a banker have a cold heart? On many levels, it is a phrase that cannot be comprehended by Joel.

Joel serves as a reminder to me to avoid several things in conversation with him—analogies, metaphors, insults, and poor humor! The easiest level for quick understanding is literal, direct, concrete, and mostly positive. This is a pattern that works best in conversation with most autistic children.

The next morning, when we ventured outside, I looked at Joel and said, "Brrr . . . it sure is cold." He said with a grin, "It's colder than an Eskimo." I'm guessing he thought of that and was anxious to use it. Truth is that his metaphor made sense, whereas mine really did not!

Tip:

There are several good Children's books on idioms and figures of speech that explain the meaning and origin of strange-sounding expressions (i.e., let the cat out of the bag, opening a can of worms, I'll put a bug in his ear, something smells fishy, a wolf in sheep's clothing).

One evening, Joel mentioned that he would like to go eat Mexican food for dinner. This was not an unusual request, since Joel could live his life eating chips and salsa with great gusto and joyous, unbridled happiness. But after he gave his request, I smiled and said, "That sounds good, and I am happy that Mexican food floats your boat." This comment resulted in a very peculiar look of confusion from Joel and reminded me of the issue of literal interpretation.

One of the typical characteristics of autism is the inability to understand subtleties and expressions. This has caused many years of clarifying, restatement, and some humorous situations. I recall the time when Joel ate three hamburgers while watching his younger brother play basketball. After the game, while we were driving home, I asked Joel if he had a hollow leg. A few minutes later, I saw Joel tapping on his leg, and I finally asked him what he was doing. He turned to me and asked, "Which one of my legs is hollow?"

We have learned to qualify our language and be more precise with our meanings. Often, though, we forget and use creative language to fit the situation. When Jordan went to college, he told us about being in a large marching band of 285 students. After asking him if the director knew his name, Jordan responded that the director knew him but probably not his name due to having "so many of us." Joel quickly and rather quizzically asked, "There are 285 Jordans?"

One big mistake was telling Joel that deer meat could cause him to grow horns on his head. I intended it as a moment of humor, a way to be silly and enjoy eating the venison. But he then started feeling his head for the horns and refused to eat deer meat until I convinced him it was a joke. This convincing took many years. Another time, he was talking on my cell phone to my wife, and after the call, I told him, "Hang up the phone." He tried desperately to actually hang the phone on different items in the car before I realized what he was doing and weakly explained that, "Hang up the phone," does not actually mean to hang up the phone.

We have explained the phrases, "money doesn't grow on trees," and, "a New York minute," and, "slow as a seven year itch," and, "dry as a bone," and, "squeaky clean," and, "Did you get up on the wrong side of the bed?" One of the most confusing was, "You could end up in the doghouse!" For Joel, all these and more need explanation and clarifying, while words and phrases which we take for granted and that everyone understands often require deciphering and a clear definition.

In the end, it has become an enjoyable family game to be exact, clear, precise, and kind in our language and in our treatment of each other. For Joel, we are literal, loving, and without excessive loquaciousness. We do this for Joel, and, as always, it is worth it.

Tip:

Be very specific on directions and limit requests to three or so steps. For example, instead of saying, "Clean your room," say, "Go to your room; put your dirty clothes in the hamper; put your shoes in the closet, and put your toys in the toy box." You may even follow up with, "Remember—clothes, shoes, toys." This could also be written down and checked off as each item is completed.

Ten

ABECEDARIAN—
It's About the Order

Gifts come to us in many shapes and sizes . . . and sometimes in ways that we least expect. Although Joel has many challenges, he also has many gifts. We discovered Joel's prowess with the alphabet when he was taken to an eye doctor at the age of three. The doctor presented the simplest chart he could find and instructed Joel to simply point in which direction the E was going. The doctor pointed to the backwards E, and Joel said, "3"! The doctor looked at Joel curiously and pointed to the E facing down. Joel promptly said, "M"! The doctor then quickly pointed to the E facing up, and Joel said, "W", and the doctor responded with, "Why don't we use the adult chart with regular letters?" From that point on, the test went much better.

In spite of being autistic, or maybe because of it, Joel has developed his lettering and spelling skills to a high achievement level. Give him time and a computer, and he can correctly spell any word pronounced correctly. When allowed to have an aid to keep him on task and allowed to use a computer, Joel has either won or come in second place on most spelling contests.

In first grade, Joel was able to write his name from right to left and left to right at the same time with both hands. He is able to see the entire alphabet in his mind so that he instantly knows how many letters a word has or a sentence. He quickly orders words and letters based on his unique image of the alphabet and how words are put together. Ordering numbers and letters is not simply a gift but is almost perfection for him. He never makes a mistake in shelving books or alphabetizing anything, so he is an invaluable asset to any library.

He can say the alphabet in any order and instantly knows when something is spelled wrong on paper. This has caused problems occasionally, because he does not hesitate to correct people when they misspell a word. He does not correct people out of arrogance but rather simply to, "make it right." Thankfully, he has many times helped me out before I sent a letter or a paper.

In addition to Joel's unusual spelling abilities, he also rarely forgets a name or details about a person. He memorizes facts that have little meaning to us but, for whatever reason, have great meaning to him. He will often ask a stranger if he or she is married, their children's names, their relative's names, and sometimes . . . even their weight.

Although his short-term memory is severely challenged, his long-term memory is exceptional. He will remember people and events from many years before and often uses that knowledge to help him in current situations.

We often rely on Joel's gifts and find ourselves baffled by him but also proud of him. We believe that there is a place in the world for Joel and that the world is better off because of him.

Joel thinks in pictures, and he places everything in some sort of order. This is true in almost all instances, from packing for a trip, to the words to music, to eating food. He orders his world, forcing it into a system that makes sense to him. Rather than responding to the needs of his senses, he responds to his unique need to have things prescribed and organized. This does not mean that he is devoid of senses, but it does mean that the sensing is established as something familiar and orderly. New and unidentified smells concern him, and events outside his mental framework are uncomfortable. A word not normally used becomes associated with a similar word, thus giving it absolution and a purpose from which to draw.

One day, after work at the downtown public library, Joel seemed somewhat agitated and uncomfortable with his current state of affairs. For some reason, this particular day at the library resulted in his having to shelve around 120 books. A normal day at the library involves around 40 books, so 120 is way beyond the expectation. Because of the volume of books, Joel did not complete his assignment until about 4:30, which is approximately 1 1/2 hours later than usual. His initial plan to practice organ at 3:30 was altered by the excessive amount of work to do at the library. In his irritated state, he demanded to practice organ although it was time to go home. The time issue was not as important as the need to keep things in sequence.

Later that evening, when he was much calmer, I mentioned to him that he had seemed quite flustered after work. He thought for a minute and said that he did not agree with me. He then said that he was a word with ten letters rather than nine. After thinking through that odd statement, I asked him, "If you aren't flustered, then what are you?" He smiled and said he was frustrated. I then counted the letters in the word 'frustrated' and discovered that all my fingers were used up, revealing that, indeed, the word 'frustrated' has ten letters.

As I processed this unusual conversation, it occurred to me that perhaps Joel knows the number of letters in words that are spoken. I then asked him the number of letters in several long words, and he responded quickly and accurately in all cases. The words that Joel says and hears from others are categorized in terms of the number of letters. He sees the words in his mind according to their length before applying meaning. It is an odd and probably useless skill, but it does signify how Joel listens and learns. This helps us as parents who are seeking to help him cope in a difficult world.

He thinks in pictures, shapes, and in sequence, working to put things in order and making things fit the puzzle piece before making sense of it. While we tend to see the larger picture and then put the pieces in place, Joel cannot always see the larger picture but can understand the individual pieces. Approaching conversations in more minute and specific ways means Joel can grasp the purpose of the word or sentence, which, in turn, allows him a quicker understanding of the concept. This is good to know, as we continue to train him to take care of himself as much as possible.

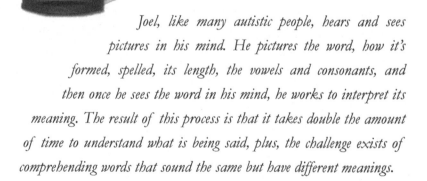

Joel, like many autistic people, hears and sees pictures in his mind. He pictures the word, how it's formed, spelled, its length, the vowels and consonants, and then once he sees the word in his mind, he works to interpret its meaning. The result of this process is that it takes double the amount of time to understand what is being said, plus, the challenge exists of comprehending words that sound the same but have different meanings.

Eleven

Cures for Autism

I attended a large conference on autism. In attendance were over 2,000 people ranging from physicians, diagnosticians, counselors, psychologists, parents, teachers, and administrators. There were also many exhibits from various companies and organizations demonstrating the vast array of resources available to schools and parents to help with autism. Although much of it dealt with awareness, some of it was also related to practical applications and recommendations for reaching autistic students.

In one notable session, a well-known physician detailed the many different treatments for autism and discussed the various tests often administered by experts to determine the level of autism in a child. He explained the secretin "miracle cure", the gamma globulin cure, the auditory awareness system, the benefits of vitamins, and he discussed the advantages and disadvantages of blood tests, IQ tests, behavioral tests, and personality profiling tests. He mentioned that while all tests can reveal certain kinds of weaknesses, there is really only one foolproof test that is always correct—a mother's opinion.

A test is designed to discern the areas that are outside the norms. Averages are determined through years of study and are, at best, simply general ideas that have limited value in labeling or prescribing the future for a child. Instead, this particular physician has found that the instincts and perceptions of a mother are right and should always be given consideration.

Those pervicacious physicians who solely rely on so-called empirical evidence may need to rethink their position and seek after the person who knows the child best—the mother. The mother is usually right, and while she may or may not have the medical or scientific background necessary to provide definitive scholarly application, her perceptions of her child are correct and should be honored.

It cannot be overemphasized that teachers, administrators, counselors, therapists, psychologists, physicians, and employers need to look to the mother for help and advice in dealing with an autistic child. While a mother does not have all the answers, she is relentless in her pursuit of what is best and what is right for her children. She should not be dismissed out of hand, and her views should always be sought in all matters related to the autistic child. She may be tainted at times, seeing only the good and hoping for the best, but even in her rose-colored glasses, she knows what is best for the child. After all, her knowledge goes back nine months prior to anyone else's contact with the child. When doubts arise, which happens often, refer to the mother for help.

In the case of our son, Joel, I am reminded to trust the instincts of Joel's mother, for nothing is greater, more personal, and more special than the love and attention of a mother to her children. Joel is fortunate to have the unconditional and devoted concern of his mother.

After reading the article titled, "The Hawthorne Effect—Why Parents Swear By Ineffective Treatments For Autism," by Sydney Spiesel, I feel compelled to respond with an explanation. Parents of autistic children are willing, through relentless and dedicated efforts, to try an infinite number of ways to help their children. This is very simply due to one truth: parents love their children and will sacrifice nearly anything to help them.

When a parent eventually realizes and accepts the disability of his/her child, a process that can unfortunately take years, the next step is to seek a cure or at least find ways to alleviate the complex and difficult situation caused by this disability. Each morning, many parents awaken with an emotional mix of optimism, love, and despair that this day will bring some kind of improvement in behavior, learning, and response from their child. What begins as a problem that will be alleviated tomorrow slowly demonstrates itself to be long term. Yet, perhaps a change in diet, environment, or medicine will be the "magic" cure for the problem.

Even as I write these words I am conflicted. I know, logically, that the cure for autism will be found by the mathematicians in the laboratories poring through millions and zillions of strands of DNA, looking for those anomalies that cause learning and social problems. Yet, I personally cannot contribute to this process, due to my lack of experience and training. So, instead of waiting patiently for the scientists to tell me what is wrong, I seek to solve the problem myself. I do this by doing what I do best . . . by loving my child and sacrificing everything to help him.

And, truthfully, almost anything we do or try makes some kind of difference. In some ways, it is a variation on the placebo effect by proxy. When the parent wants something enough to pay for it, to sacrifice for it, to study it, or to make a journey, then it just may happen. This kind of projected desire for improvement often makes its way to the child, resulting in positive improvement for everyone. Unfortunately, it is often short-term growth. Yet, the glimmer of hope and joy is vastly beneficial to the parents of the disabled child.

But before sounding cynical, I must interject that many of the cures are indeed helpful. Good nutrition, for one, is always valuable. Vitamins, if used judiciously, are also good for the body. Exercise, breathing techniques, and conditioning are all good practices to consider. Behavior modification and rewards for good behavior are standard operating procedure for parents, and all efforts at understanding behavior are helpful. So I urge parents to continue to find answers and to try myriad and sundry ways to help their children. In the end, it is all about love and sacrifice. We seek answers because we care; to do otherwise is not an option.

An autism conference is one of the most enlightening experiences a parent can have. Exhibits, sessions, recommendations, suggestions, and unlimited ideas abound, with each one expounding the benefits of a particular method for helping autistic children. I attended and examined each method as thoroughly as possible, seeking, like all the other parents, an answer to helping my child, Joel, autistic since birth.

Each method has the distinction of being helpful, if not for itself but at the very least for the placebo effect (which cannot be denied or ignored for its validity). Parents are not wrong to explore and commit themselves to examining each method with the idea of finding the "magic" cure for autism. But, sadly, it will not be found. There is no magic cure for the disability. This truth, however, does not preclude the amazing benefits of each method. Parents need to know for themselves how each system helps. Vitamins, nutrition, behavior modification, Hyperbolic, exercise, physical therapy, speech therapy, reading specialists, music therapy, and a host of medications are just some of the necessary procedures for helping your autistic child.

But, in the end, there are two things that should never be forgotten, and these two things are interrelated: 1) never give up on your child and believe in him or her, and 2) take seriously the unparalleled and ubiquitous instincts of a mother for her children. Obviously, there are bad mothers in the world and awful situations which prevent autistic children from being loved by their parents, but, for most children, there is a woman who loves them in spite of their challenges and who will never give up trying to help them. With this devoted and cherished love will come instincts for motherhood that should always be considered at the very top of the methods for helping autistic children.

Mothers know when their children are seriously ill, emotionally distraught, putting on an act, frightened, joyful, developing a problem, or need to eat. They know when children are teething, have a diaper problem, are struggling in a relationship, are resentful, or excited, wary, cautious, or too accepting. There is a bond between a mother and her child that nothing can sever. The instinctual feelings that a mother has for what her child needs and what he or she is experiencing is so strong as to be nearly supernatural. The synergy is often so closely tied as to create a projection of success in spite of contrary evidence. In other words, a mother is often desperate enough for her child to progress that she can cause progress by sheer desire. This is the power of the placebo effect in improving disabled children.

Obviously, the placebo effect does not have long-range gain, but even short-term improvement speaks volumes for the method. So to the dads throughout the world: when you are in doubt as to what is wrong with the child, turn to the mom. She probably has a good idea and likely knows the best treatment. This message is for physicians as well.

Twelve

The Siblings

What parent would turn down a cry for help from a son or daughter? The answer is easy—no parent. When your child needs you, you are there for him. At times, you might make the decision to delay the help as a teaching tool or to encourage self-reliance or individual choice, yet, in the end, you provide the love and support needed.

Joel, however, has an unusual support base in his cry for help. Joel is fortunate to have two brothers who look out for him, two brothers who guide him, two brothers who love him, and two brothers who help him. His older brother, Jacob, balances the need to teach Joel independence, while also offering him appropriate help when necessary. Jacob always drops what he is doing to listen to Joel, and he is very quick to take him places, talk to him, and help him with his homework. Jacob is consistently patient with Joel and is dedicated to providing him with a warm, loving, brotherly environment. Not that Jacob is always easy on Joel. Jacob works to teach him independence, appropriate behavior, conversational ease, priorities, and time management. Jacob recognizes the vast influence he has over Joel and uses that knowledge in a multitude of positive ways.

Jordan, three years younger than Joel, has had a little rougher time adjusting to having an autistic brother. Joel towers above him, and, until recently, Joel has been stronger and faster than

Jordan. And Jordan has viewed autism as primarily a behavioral issue, rather than a neurological, sociological, and educational one. Although Joel wants to spend time with Jordan, he does not know how to play normal games or have normal conversations, which then results in a type of pestering behavior that is annoying and irritating. Yet, as Jordan continues to mature physically and emotionally, he finds himself in a position of helping, guiding, and mentoring Joel. Jordan's inherent creativity finds fruition in developing alternative means of communication and brotherly activities. It is always a joy to see Joel and Jordan interacting in a multitude of positive ways.

All three brothers are very protective of each other in all situations. Jacob and Jordan are always watching out for Joel, insuring that people treat him well and that he is not creating any kind of problem for himself. I always smile when I see a glare from Jacob toward anyone giving the appearance of not treating Joel well. The boys have an unusual bond that can be attributed to living under an umbrella of love and trust and dealing with the constant challenges of autism. Their love and patience with Joel is evident at home, at church, at school, and at social situations. With this patience and understanding has come a strong, compassionate altruism for those less fortunate and for those with learning problems.

The cry for help from Joel is answered by his brothers through their devoted attention to his development. But, ironically, the ultimate help once again is Joel helping them. For in their work to offer Joel patience, love, trust, and guidance, they inadvertently grow in character and substance. The intertwining of lives through selfless giving to those in need is mutually beneficial to everyone. Jacob and Jordan are better people because of Joel, and Joel is fortunate to have two of the greatest brothers a person could ever have.

Thirteen

Mysteries of Lying and Cheating

He cannot tell a lie. No, he is not George Washington or honest Abe Lincoln; he is Joel Tucker. His affliction/gift prevents him from applying creative thinking to situations. Lying is a creative endeavor in that it takes an actively creative mind to fabricate and elaborate. Joel states the facts without embellishment.

We can always depend on Joel to express the events as they happened or at least what he saw and experienced. He does not assume things and does not tell anything that he only thinks might have happened. Like the old TV show *Dragnet*, he sticks to the facts and often expresses them without any emotion. Joel's world is somewhat pleasantly superficial, in that he does not imagine the abstract or pretend to know something that is not there. He lives in the concrete world of the five senses without anticipation of what those senses will be. He responds in truth to what he sees and does not interpret beyond the obvious.

This results in extreme reliability of events and situations without the typical guesswork found in most people's views. We tend to rely on the perceptions and interpretations of individuals rather than strictly on the facts. Joel, however, provides us with a reliable account of his experiences. It is both comforting and frightening for us as parents. I am often glad that Joel does not see or sense any criticism or even anything negative around him. This causes him to have a pleasant demeanor and causes him to find the best in everyone and in everything.

On the other hand, it is a little unnerving to know that Joel does not sense any danger or possible threats around him. While Joel brings an eternal optimism with him in his responses to people and events, the truth is that not all experiences and not all people are well-intentioned. This keeps us and Joel's brothers on guard to insure that any threats, whether veiled or obvious, are quelled and that Joel is protected.

But we do not necessarily desire to change Joel into a lying, suspicious, darkly questioning individual. There is enough of that in the world already. Instead, while we do wish to instill in Joel the ability to discern and recognize differences in people and situations, we hope to retain the goodness and joy that he emanates everywhere he goes.

This is probably Joel's greatest gift . . . to transform the world around him and to spread joy infectiously to other people. A great writer will work linearly to provide congruity and concinnity to his prose. Like a great writer who speaks with the pen or the keyboard, Joel's personality and comportment are beyond reproach, and his natural magnetic charm joyously infects every room he enters. Never a braggadocio, he won't boast, bluster, or exult himself in any fashion. He is not capable of exaggeration, hyperbole, or self-absorption in the way we normally define it. His acts of selfishness are to serve his own need to meet people, love people, affirm people, and help people.

Joel's unusual gifts of honesty and unlimited powers of love set him apart from the rest of world and make him unequivocally special. In a world replete with fear, suspicion, caution, prejudice, and judgment, Joel escapes into a world complete with love, goodness, acceptance, tolerance, and trust.

Sitting at the dinner table, ready to eat a delicious but also typical meal of chips and hot sauce, rice, beans, nachos, and tacos, the topic, after having exhausted discussions of national politics and religious philosophy, turned to the events of the day. Between chips loaded with hot sauce, nachos with cheese, guacamole, and sour cream, we heard a rather dark tale of a small first-grade boy, who, in an effort to get ahead, had taken a set of tickets from the teacher's desk and then lied about the theft. He claimed to have found the tickets in his desk by saying that they had suddenly "shown up". When questioned, he finally admitted to the theft, the lie, and the desire to cheat the other students. It was not a good moment for the little boy.

In the discussion that evening, we tried to determine the cause for the event, including the general character of the student, the student's family background, the circumstances of the day, the position of the moon in the sky, the upcoming weather change, the sinful nature of man, the lack of accountability in our modern world, the effects of media on human behavior, the disintegrating moral fiber of our current culture, and the inevitable "kids these days" cliché. Following this enlightening conversation, we entered into various ideas for appropriate punishment with the goal of how to deter future negative behavior. Several suggestions were put forth involving physical pain, hard labor, formal apologies, suspension, time-out, and various deprivation methods. In this enjoyable conversation, we turned to Joel to get his view of the best punishment.

Joel, who was seventeen at the time, did not know how to relate to this conversation. The whole concept of someone who would lie, cheat, or steal was difficult, or maybe even impossible, for Joel to envision. Furthermore, to fabricate an appropriate set of consequences for such an action was completely beyond the scope of his thought processes. After realizing that Joel had

55

not understood most of our conversation, I asked him what he thought would happen to him if he were to lie, cheat, or steal.

The unusual expression that was on his face is difficult to describe. It was something akin to confusion but with more emotion behind it. I was a bit surprised, since Joel tends to express his thoughts without much emotion. His face revealed a form of determination and conviction, as he made the statement, "It will never happen. I will never do any of those things." We laughed, knowing that a person who makes such a statement is probably lying to himself. While we, as civilized human beings, have a desire to behave according to the law legislated by the government and hopefully use important documents such as the Bible as the authoritative written word guiding our moral framework, it remains difficult to uphold a high standard of expectation in all situations.

One can not help but be moved by the story of Jean Valjean, the protagonist in Victor Hugo's marvelous novel *Les Miserables*, who was sentenced to nineteen years of hard labor for stealing a loaf of bread in order to feed his starving family. Although it feels unjust to us to punish him for something he did out of necessity and out of compassion, at the same time, we justify this in our minds by acknowledging that he did, indeed, commit a crime. Did the punishment far exceed the crime? Certainly. Did he more than pay for his mistake? No question about that. And yet, his initial crime was a crime of choice, in that he made the decision to take the bread while knowing the possible consequences of his actions.

Joel does not have the ability to make those choices. He knows the rules and follows them. The rules of stealing, lying, or cheating are mysteries to him, due to these acts not existing in his experience. Because of this, he cannot devise an appropriate punishment. The laws of cause and effect, in the case of breaking the rules, are not in Joel's emotional makeup. He cannot fathom a punishment, since he does not comprehend the crime. His innocence is not necessarily out of choice but rather because of his natural character. The rest of us often have to work at doing the right thing; for Joel, it is easy.

Fourteen

Following the Rules

In this oddly chaotic world, we often find moments of order and form, and these moments give us objective rules that can be comforting in a systematic way. Although my generally free-spirited and independent nature is rewarded through music, literature, and different adventures, at the same time, I recognize the vast benefits of governance and prescription. Somewhere there is a balance of free creativity versus systematized rigidity, and as we journey through life, we hope to achieve symmetry in our expectations for the waves of experiences thrown in our pathway each day.

Joel, however, often demands order and rule-following as a system of life and organization. Some of this is born out of his trust of authority, and some of this, unfortunately, is a reflection of his lack of creative thinking. And, yet, despite its being a stereotypical characteristic of autism, the demand for order and rule-following is a charming trait and one that bears modeling. If the sign says turn, then you must turn. If the rule states to cross at the crosswalk, then you had better not do otherwise.

Recently, at a formal dinner, there were name tags placed for seating. Unfortunately, the person who was supposed to sit across from me at this long, rectangular table did not attend the event, which then left a seat empty. Joel's name tag had been placed at the chair next to the empty seat. Joel, of course, insisted on sitting where his tag was located, even after I invited him to sit across from me in the empty chair. After thinking about it, I exchanged the name tags, thereby making him comfortable in changing seats. Despite the fact that he had seen me move the name tags, he was happy to oblige, and we enjoyed the rest of the evening.

The following day, Joel and I ate at a nice restaurant together, and as we prepared to leave, I noticed a door with an exit sign and another door with an enter sign. As we neared the doors, the enter door opened with a couple entering the restaurant. Due to the efficiency of the open door, I chose to leave the restaurant through that door—but Joel remained inside. As the door shut behind me, I noticed that Joel was not with me. I went back into the restaurant and saw Joel standing with his finger pointing at the exit door.

The hostess was looking at him oddly, and I said it would take too long to explain. We both then left through the exit door with a happy Joel and perplexed looks on the faces of the other people. Joel followed the rules and was satisfied. He often reminds us to observe the speed limit, the red lights, the stop signs, the parking signs, and all the other myriad rules that help govern our behavior. In the library, he quickly but deliberately places the books in the sequential order that is needed. Conversely, he is not comfortable in a chaotic environment and does not respond well to subjectivity or even an excess of emotions.

In Joel's embracing of order, rules, and direction, he, in turn, avoids the ataxia, or the lack of order which is often found in large social circles and in certain environments. He seeks to order his world and grows concerned when all is not as it should be. In many ways, Joel's desire for objectivity is often refreshing and reminds us that chaos is ultimately nihilistic and that cultural growth occurs through order . . . not confusion. Let us choose times to attack ataxia and respect the Joels of the world.

Tip:

Chores/routines that are problematic can be converted into a game. Try racing with siblings to take a fast shower or get dressed. Try beating the timer to get a prize. Any kind of fun contest often becomes a catalyst for success.

Fifteen

Amaranthine Angels

My position on angels and their existence was asked of me the other day. I answered that I believe in them but that I do not understand them. Having a somewhat cautious, suspicious nature, with leanings toward cynicism, my believing in angels does not come lightly or easily, yet there are events which are difficult to label and impossible to define that seem to be undeniably guided by unseen forces and shaped by mystery and magic. Acknowledging such forces which operate outside the realm of the sensing reality that encompasses our perception is antithetical to the power philosophy we love to embrace. In other words, we like to think that we are in control of all facets of our life. But, in truth, we are not. There are simply too many unexplained events that demonstrate how little control we actually have.

This does not mean that we are devoid of free will or that the concept of choice and human experience is all predetermined, but it does mean that overt and external circumstances cannot always be planned or ordered in advance. It has been said that we are shaped by events, that our reactions define our character, and that life happens when we are making other plans. Be that as it may, superior minds have dealt with the concept of free will without any kind of conclusion, and it is my contention that our daily activities belong to us, to an extent, but that our destiny is not our own. I am comfortable in this hybrid zone of free will and choice versus pre-determinacy and lack of free will. A theologian (which I am not) would say it is Arminianism versus Calvinism. For me, a utilitarian (at least for now, until I find another term to describe my oddly eclectic philosophy of the world), I prefer to accept those strange but joyous events as being glorious yet sporadic divergences exhibited and practiced by angels with some sort of higher functional and pragmatic application.

We, the Tucker family, have kept them busy over the years, maybe even to an exhaustive level. One rather dramatic incident occurred when Joel was three years old. He was dropped off at a friend's house, while my wife, who was expecting our third child, went to her prenatal checkup. The house was newly constructed, with two stories, and included a children's game room on the 2nd story. Because of the fire code, windows were required to be easily opened from the inside. Unfortunately, this meant that a firm push on any window would result in that window opening. As the children were playing, Joel leaned back against the window, which caused it to open, and he fell from the window, all the way to the ground two stories below.

All the children and neighbors heard the cry for help and rushed outside only to see Joel lying on the ground crying. Because of the potential disaster, everyone was afraid to move him for fear of adding problems to any broken bones. My wife Clairissa coincidentally drove up a few minutes later, saw the crowd, and asked what was wrong. Upon hearing her voice, Joel got up and ran, yes—ran to her, sobbing. She embraced him, and in a broken voice, the owner of the home said tearfully that he had fallen from the 2nd story window. Clairissa immediately put him in the car and took him to the pediatrician for X-rays. Aside from a scratch on his back from the windowsill, there were no other injuries. He was not hurt at all, and within a short time, he was back to being his same rambunctious self.

As I reflect on this incident, I remain convinced that an angel's hand gently lowered Joel to the ground and offered him protection and comfort. He is surrounded by angels who often have to work diligently to keep him safe from harm. And that is why I believe in angels. I do not understand them. I cannot see them. I do not know anything about them. I do not know if there are many or just a few of them, or whether they are large or small, male or female, but I am comforted to know that they watch out for Joel. We will do our part to keep them from having to work too hard, but in those few rare cases, I appreciate their willingness to step in. I do know this: they are timeless, eternal, ever-present, and with a beautiful, amaranthine, forever quality that defies explanation.

Sixteen

Fear: An Unknown Emotion

There is a marvelous, though disturbing story by the Brothers Grimm of a boy who left home to find fear, to get the creeps. He was unable to fear, unable to shudder, and had never experienced getting the creeps. In his travels and adventures, the boy continues to feel no fear of anything. Horror, fright, terror, and mishap are visited upon him, but to no avail. He cannot seem to summon from anywhere within himself the emotion of fear or the creeps. He does not know or understand the elements which cause fear, and he, therefore, is desensitized to the possibility. To shiver or shudder or quake over something is an unknown experience.

But, at the end of the story, a bucket of wet minnows was poured all over him. He shuddered, and shivered, and finally learned what the creeps were. He was thankful for this emotion, and the story concludes rather humorously.

For Joel, autism has prevented him from having a natural understanding of fear. His inclination is to be afraid of nothing and never experience the emotion of fear or the feeling of the creeps.

While it could be argued that many fears are learned either from socialization or from actual events, some fears, no doubt, are instinctual, such as the fear of falling, of getting run over, the fear of extreme heat, the danger of certain animals, or even the fear of people. But, for Joel, with his natural trust of all things and all people, he tends rarely to consider danger or even react with any kind of apprehension at all. Our natural instinct to look out for him due to his lack of awareness of danger has added to his innocent acceptance of all things good. Yet what parent would place an autistic child in harm's way to teach him that dangers do exist? Would the lesson even work for an autistic child? Likely . . . it would not, for these children do not learn from experience or from the "School of Hard Knocks."

We have tried to teach Joel a healthy respect for animals, heights, heat, cold, and traffic. Over the years, we have wondered what would make Joel shudder, shake, tremble, or have trepidation. What would give Joel the creeps? So I asked him how he would react if I threw worms all over his body. He found that to be very amusing (a positive emotion that we are glad he experiences) and said, "I would say please remove the worms from my body, thank you." Unlike our protagonist in the Grimm's Fairy Tale, Joel would not get the creeps from slithery, slimy creatures all over him.

Of course, it has all been rather funny and enjoyable, but it does point to the constant need for education and responses to stimuli. Joel's quest to find the creeps is not led by himself but rather by us. In the end, who would want the creeps anyway?

Seventeen

Going to Camp—
Ringing the Bell

W e followed the young man, one of the "commanders" assigned to Joel, to the dorm to help him get settled in his new and very temporary location. We looked in the room that contained several beds already occupied, and I felt a mixture of trepidation and excitement for Joel, now seventeen, that he would be staying in this dorm for the next two nights. We opened his suitcase to remove his fluffy, warm sleeping bag, got out his favorite pillow, and placed them on the unoccupied bed which happened to be approximately in the center of the room.

Then we looked around the room. We were comforted, to an extent, by meeting some of the other campers who were similar to Joel in that all had some kind of disability, mental or physical, or a combination of both. My first impression was that Joel was among friends of various ages and various disabilities, but all of whom were charming in their limitations, special in their hunger for life, and warm in their joy and excitement. This thought created an emotional sense of confidence in the camp as we completed the introductions and prepared to leave the dorm and the center. We hugged Joel goodbye, with that same feeling all parents have throughout their lives, not unlike the mother seeing her daughter off for the first day of kindergarten, saying goodbye for the first day of college, or perhaps even that odd feeling of elation mixed with loving concern as the young couple heads off on their honeymoon. *Will Joel be okay? Will he have fun? Will he learn? Will he need us? Will he eat right? Will he sleep?* All normal parenting thoughts.

It was Camp Mission Possible, not 'Impossible' as Joel reminded us countless times, located at the 4-H Center at Lake Brownwood. The camp was complete with a playground, climbing wall, swimming pool, shooting range, cafeteria, offices, dorms, canoes, and plenty of space for playing and learning. There were plenty of sponsors, adults, and students called "commanders" to ensure the safety and success of each attendee. The schedule was rigid in its specific details on expectations, including bedtime, meals, events, rules, discipline, and code of conduct, but the love and compassion seemed to have no boundaries, for it oozed freely and unconditionally from the directors, sponsors, and commanders (who were not really commanders but rather facilitators or caregivers).

Two days later, which felt like two months in many ways and two hours in others, we returned to the 4-H Center to pick up Joel and see the final event, a video of all the campers and their experiences. It was easy to see our tall son in the front row, as we entered the large but darkened room. The music began and included inspirational music as we watched the video of each camper climb, shoot, run, dance, fish, and swim. Among the most touching pictures were the shots of the campers as they were carefully strapped in for the climbing wall where they reached to the stars with each step and each grip . . . and were gently pulled up by the attached ropes to ring the bell at the top of the wall.

After the video, we gathered up Joel's belongings, and following many thanks and hugs for and from many people, we returned home with our son 'The hero who had rung the bell.' The bell rings loud and clear for all the special children in the world and for those who help them achieve the impossible. Ask not for whom the bell tolls—it tolls for them.

As I read the paper, watch the news, and learn about bombs, death, suicide, drugs, terrorism, and destruction, I remind myself that the darkness of the world does not come from the hearts of the special children. The light of the world shines brightly for them and for the many who reach out to help them ring the bell. Thank you, 4-H Center and Camp Mission Possible for making the dreams come true. May your bell ring loudly, clearly, joyfully, and beautifully for all to hear.

Eighteen

Creativity and Music

To define the character traits of a musician is to limit and even endanger the creative individuality of the human spirit that creates, interprets, and expresses the many facets of what music means and the emotion surrounding the creation and enjoyment of sound. But, indeed, and rather strangely, there are some general characteristics often found in many musicians, such as emotionalism, spontaneity, complexity, which are not displayed by our son Joel, and he loves music as much as anyone.

Most musicians, performers, composers, appreciators, and scholars have an element of creativity and expression that requires emotional demonstration in some form or another. According to Aristotle, music helps purify and organize unwanted emotions by reaching into the brain and beyond, into the soul of the human, and then clarifying and sometimes systematizing those feelings that are difficult to put into words. Music, and the arts in general, allow for expression of emotions which, in turn, purify or provide catharsis for the human spirit.

Joel may not have all the typical characteristics of autism; incidentally, in fact, very few autistic children have absolutely all the qualities that traditionally define autism, but he does have two distinguishable traits often found in children with his disability: Joel displays a marked lack of emotional personal creativity, and connected to this is an unusual objective expression of truth without emotional coloring. This enchanting and unusual quality requires him always to tell the truth in all situations without any additional human interpretation or supplementation of the situation. Joel seeks after joy, goodness, and light in all things and in all people without an awareness of any darkness that may exist in the world or any kind of hidden agenda. He finds the good in everyone and everything.

Because music demands emotional expression, it becomes a difficult but not impossible medium for Joel to understand and to apply. Yet, music is very meaningful to Joel in many ways despite the fact that he is unable to sing. His two favorite styles of music are the Hymn and the March, both of which are clean and organized styles of music without the romantic, emotional excesses found in other genres. A majority of hymns are in four to eight measure phrases with a repeated chorus, in a balanced poetic meter, with emphasis on the text, and mostly a singable, tuneful melody. Similarly, a march with its introduction, first strain repeated, second strain repeated, trio, break strain, and repeated trio, maintains a sense of balance, tonality, rhythmic energy, and melodic tunefulness. Both genres are organized, obvious, clean, enjoyable, uncomplicated, and musically pure.

Joel's inability to pass negative judgment prevents him from criticizing other types of music, such as Jazz, Country Western, Rock, or atonality, but he does display marked appreciation and emotional response to hymns and marches. Furthermore, he loves hearing the organ playing almost anything. Psychologically, Joel seems to desire a consonant, dissonant-free existence without the edginess and discomfort that are often a part of the ups and downs of normal living. An extension of this desire is the smooth, non-percussiveness of the organ playing hymns and the light, enjoyable quality of marches.

Harmonically, most marches and most hymns are in a major key, giving them a buoyancy and unbounded optimism that easily match Joel's world-view and his desire for a harmonious existence. Since most people tend to respond and appreciate music that matches their own philosophy, personality, and value system, it is easy to understand how hymns and marches being played on the organ are a manifestation of Joel's own charm, warmth, and positive outlook on life. In Joel's world, the more hymns and marches that are heard, the better off we are! Maybe he has something there.

Upon completing the previous paragraphs on Joel, I realized that most of the attention was on Joel as a listener and an appreciator of music, but mention should be made that Joel is also a performing musician with his choice of media being the pipe organ or the electronic organ. In many ways, it is difficult to explain why he prefers the sound and style of the organ over other instruments, and it is equally difficult to understand his desire and his almost need to play hymns on an organ. Yet there is no doubt that Joel loves playing hymns on the organ.

The organ is considered the "king" of all the instruments, with its almost infinite combinations of sounds and possibilities of range and dynamic extension, not to mention the requirement to use both hands and feet in a complex display of virtuosity and musical comprehension. Organists are generally highly intelligent, detail oriented, and multi-dimensioned, with a quiet strength and self-confidence born from playing an instrument with the capability of dominating all other sound.

Unlike a piano, which relies on a pedal to provide for a sustained quality, the organ has a smooth, sustained quality that requires a special playing technique of connecting the notes by pressing the next note at the same moment the previous one is lifted. The result is a beautiful, non-percussive approach to playing that allows for great expression and elision of musical phrases.

As was mentioned in an earlier chapter, Joel's propensity to see the world "non-percussively", optimistically, and harmoniously, and his preference for smooth music without the harsh angles often found in music, is manifested in the type of music he enjoys hearing and performing. Related to this is his speech, which often lacks definition, articulation, and even volume. He intends to enunciate accurately and to speak clearly and loudly enough to be heard, but the result is often somewhat slurred, hesitant, and at a low dynamic. In an odd but not necessarily negative way, Joel's speech patterns resemble that of an organ . . . connected, non-percussive, rich, pleasant, and congenial.

I believe that Joel's preference for hymns and marches is indicative of his general positive demeanor, his desire for order, total tolerance, and acceptance of all things good. I also contend that his desire to practice the organ is an extension of his own unusual approach to speaking and his preference for connected sounds rather than angular, sharp sounds. This is, of course, difficult or maybe even impossible to prove, but, nevertheless, Joel continues to enjoy playing hymns on the organ, and he is very happy to practice for several hours a day. His tendency to repeat the same hymn in the same way will be dealt with at another time.

Despite having grown up in a family of singers, I was, unfortunately, not blessed with a beautiful singing voice. Yet I was blessed, if one can call it a blessing, with a great zeal and love of singing and with a general love of music. My somewhat nasal-sounding, rattly voice does not deter me from frequently applying my love of music, and the "natural" instrument God has given me, to a multitude of circumstances, including, but not limited to, singing in the shower, singing while driving, walking, shopping, and maybe thinking out loud (much to the chagrin of my friends). But the question on the table today is not about me but rather about Joel.

He has never sung a note. He loves music and discusses it frequently and with great interest. I smile as I think about this morning, when he said, "How about, 'I'd Do Anything'?" Not understanding his question at first, I then remembered a discussion in the car the day before when we were trying to decide the best song from the musical *Oliver*. With his enjoyment of organ music, and songs in general, comes frequent practicing on the organ and the piano, with most of the music being hymns of various types and in various keys.

So why doesn't he sing? Is it due to a fear of failure, or does he actually lack the ability to sing? I have heard a few people who could not seem to match pitch, which implies a judgment on my part, but I do not think I have encountered someone who simply cannot do it. Obviously, a person without the ability to speak would also lack the ability to sing, but this also brings to mind the odd cases of people who stutter when they speak but can sing without hesitation (Mel Tillis and Carly Simon to name two). Yet those people, and there are many, can and do sing with success and, more importantly, enjoyment. The obvious answer to this mystery is that singing requires a slightly different part of the brain than speaking. But is it really that simple?

There has been much research relating psychology and singing that reference the benefits of singing for mental health, for physiological gain, and for the general peace and welfare of the individual countenance. I find this to be generally true for most people. Singing is a creative venture that requires memory, expression, emotional cognition, depth of thought, a sensitive awareness of the environment, and a sense of goal-direction and purpose. We sing as an expression of our feelings, our deepest thoughts, our emotions, and as a way to put shape and form to our joys, our fears, our optimism, and our sorrows. Singing does all that and more. But, coincidentally and unfortunately, the act of singing uses all the faculties that are missing or weakened in autism—a disability that tends to affect the ability for creative expression of emotions.

Joel does feel what we feel and experience what we experience, but when he tries to express those events in an emotional way, he gets blocked by the weakness in the central nervous system, the area of the brain that allows and encourages the outer expression of feelings. He cannot sing, because he cannot demonstrate his deepest emotions. Are they in him? Yes, without a doubt. He cares; he fears; he loves; he worries; he reaches out, and he is comfortable in his skin. But he cannot sing, and while it is hard to understand, it is simply a characteristic that makes him who he is—Joel Tucker.

For me, it happens nearly every day. For others, it may just be once a week or every now and then. Nearly everyone I have known or have met inevitably gets a song on his mind that won't seem to leave. In fact, there are techniques used for getting songs off the mind, including singing "Jingle Bells", watching a sports show, or going to sleep. For many people, however, the song returns to haunt our thoughts and responses. Although usually pleasant, occasionally a song stays in our head which we may not even enjoy. Most songs in the mind are rather simplistic, catchy, memorable, and may include Folk songs, Broadway, Christian, Rock, Country, or even Classical themes. While the song on the mind may be maddening, in many ways the song is also cathartic and keeps our emotions in check. The power of music as an abstract art form is still to be completely understood.

Driving down the road with Joel in the passenger seat, I found myself singing, "The Lusty Month of May" from *Camelot*. The melody is catchy, and the pure joy of the song is infectious, causing an expressive response of happiness. I was humming, tapping, singing, and shaking, when Joel said, "Dad, I have never had a song on my mind."

This quieted me considerably as I pondered his statement. Joel's autism causes a significant lack of creative ability. Jacob and Jordan both experienced imaginary friends as small children, and Jordan especially had an imaginary world which we found to be very entertaining at times. Yet Joel never experienced an imaginary friend, thereby implying that he either does not express his imagination or does not have one.

For music to be in the mind, imagination is required in some form or another. Without an imagination, the abstract art of music cannot lodge inside the mind. Joel's autism prevents the creative spark generated by the imagination, resulting in a marked lack of conceptual thinking, leading to the lack of song in his mind. This does not mean that Joel is deprived of the beauty and joy of music, but it does mean that he is perhaps missing both the burden and the liberation of emotions that music can provide.

Ironically, we learn something about ourselves from autism. We are dependent upon our imagination, and we benefit from what is inside our brains, conceptually and creatively. Yet it is not an essential part of our lives. In the way that a blind person compensates for his blindness, autism compensates for the missing creativity. And in the way a blind person does not necessarily miss what he has never had (Maybe he doesn't miss sight, but he certainly does wonder.) and therefore leads the fulfilled life he knows, so also does an autistic lead the life he knows—a life without imagination (at least from our perspective).

While it may sound like a rationalization, to a point, I contend that, in some ways, Joel's never having a song in his mind is actually liberating and strangely prevents him from the extremes of emotion or at least the range of emotions we normally experience. There is no song, but that does not mean there is no joy. His joy is expressed in other ways, and his emotions are dealt with apart from what is inside his head. This makes for an unusual existence . . . but one worth trying to understand.

Nineteen

Give Him His Moment

In the day-to-day and often murky waters of parenting, one of the toughest decisions to make is when to let the child have his way, his moment, his victory. Parents worry that giving in too much sends a message of constant capitulation and ease of life's journey, an artificial world that will inevitably cause a jarring of the senses for the maturing child. The other extreme, however, sets up an autocratic governance where a child often feels undervalued and is not permitted any kind of freedom for victory or the making of mistakes. In general, as for most parents, I subscribe to the idea of saying yes when possible and allowing children their moment within the confines of safety and security. Yet, I have often reminded my children, particularly in their younger years, that our family is not a democracy and that parents get to make the decisions apart from any kind of voting privilege children may think they have!

It comes back so often to: the balance of parenting—freedom vs restriction. Usually, the best course is somewhere in the middle, generously spiced and adorned with lots of love. One day they will be on their own, and they need to know how to make the right decision, but to understand that the love of parents is always the overriding criterion for decisions. So parents worry that saying "No" too often will result in rebelliousness, or that saying "Yes" too often will result in a loss of authority. We walk on the tightrope of parenting, hoping for the insights which will be best for the child but never sacrificing safety and security along the way.

Now, in the autistic child, all is different. The parenting skills are not the same. The philosophy is not the same, and the thought processing is not the same. Raising an autistic child is markedly different from a normal child, and the goals are unique. Do not try to assume that you can be the same parent for a normal child as you are for the autistic child. The rules have changed.

To all those who are often judgmental of the so-called "bad" parents in the world, could it be that you are observing a child with autism? Is it a child who does not live in the same world as everyone else? Perhaps it is a parent who is struggling to make the puzzle pieces fit for the child. It reminds me of the old adage, "Before you criticize someone, walk a mile in his shoes."

But parenting an autistic child is not an excuse for mediocre parenting. It is, instead, an opportunity to help a disabled child to be safe, to cope, to learn, to be successful, to see the world in its totality, to find joy in the midst of the challenges, and, yes, for the parent to feel successful as well. Too often, we forget the depth of emotional distress that the parent experiences. For a parent to feel productive, loving, and successful, he or she must experience some kind of affirmation for his or her efforts. While these affirming times are often intermittent, they can be quite euphoric.

But, unlike a normal child, the autistic child is not necessarily being trained for independence, for that unaided flight to the world. Instead, the autistic child is simply finding his niche, a way for him to fit into the world, likely with lots of help. Rather than worrying that "giving in" will somehow corrupt him forever, will not allow him to recognize authority, or will ill-prepare him for the challenges of the world, perhaps parents need to find those opportunities to allow for some degree of contentment. Give him his moment, for there are not very many of those.

Just as in raising a normal child, parents must seek a balance between exerting authority and allowing for some degree of independence. But, unlike a normal child, the battle is not for quelling rebelliousness; the battle is for making the puzzle pieces fit. In the end, safety and security are the goals, and raising a child is written on a tablet made with lots of love.

Tip:

Likely, the parents know more than any expert, doctor, counselor, teacher, or well-intentioned person. These people are helpful, and often their training and education provides great insights and benefits, and, after all, anything you learn has value. But parents, particularly mothers, generally need to trust their instincts about their children.

Twenty

The Value of Life

Imagine a world where the inherent value of an object has no intrinsic worth, no price tag, and means nothing to an individual other than its own merits. Imagine a world where money has no application and becomes useful merely for momentary satisfaction, including the sound of coins falling with the result being a soda coming from the machine. Imagine a world where the appeal for materials is based primarily on preference without regard to quality, history, potential, supply, or demand, a world without greed or envy of those who have, or, conversely, a world without pity for those who have not, and no acknowledgment of rich or poor, a world of equality, and a world without judgment.

This is Joel's world. He does not understand money. Oh, he understands the price tag on an item; he can add up the dollars and cents, and he knows that it takes money to buy things at the store. He also knows that Mom and Dad discuss money and often seem concerned about it, but in the end, he doesn't know why some things require more than others. An RC Cola out of the machine requires three quarters that make a fun sound when fed into the machine, whereas, a tie at the store needs paper money or Dad's little plastic card in his wallet.

On any given day, Joel would like a new suit or a pipe organ in the house, or a bag of chips with hot sauce. Purchasing shoes for $5 at a corner sale has the same meaning as a new pair from

Macy's. We have told him, and he can accept, that a pipe organ is not an option for our home, but that does not change his desire for one. Yet his wanting one is not a covetous obsession but is rather an idea of a given moment similar to his desire for a cola or new shoes.

The need for more money is a motivating incentive for hard work in our society and indirectly affects supply and demand, which then creates an economic culture that pervades our footsteps and our actions. Without a sense of labor and free trade, we fall into the futuristic and flawed utopian *Brave New World* of total equality and peace devoid of the human elements needed for growth and improvement. Ironically, those very elements are what lead to both happiness and misery in our world. If our happiness and joy is based upon money, which leads to a greater acquisition of wealth, then we fall into an extrinsic desire for more. In that marvelous book by Aldous Huxley, those rare moments of dissatisfaction and confusion require a "Soma" to reach a drug-induced state of happiness and false euphoria. When joy is derived from material objects, the inevitable result is an empty feeling from never having enough.

Supply and demand is a result of the inner need to improve, a drive to succeed, a necessity for affirmation, an intrinsic need for self-actualization, or a desperate requirement to be important with the acquisition of more things. It seems to be human nature to want more toys for Christmas, and we want the best and most expensive toys. Never mind that children tend to play with the boxes more than the actual toys! And yet, before falling into a diatribe on society's materialism, it is the inner drive and human spirit that has created cities and technology, and which progresses forward to greater heights of creativity. Personal ambition, dedication to labor, and self-improvement leads directly to an acknowledgment of the value of objects and the ability to make judgments of worth.

To return to Joel's world, a world without the knowledge of money and the value of objects can and does result in a lack of ambition for wealth and acquisition. This makes Joel's world rather bland and oddly confusing by our standards. The new Lexus that passes by is simply a vehicle, not to be admired more than any old Chevrolet. Given clothes, food, shelter, and a piano or organ, Joel is happy. He does not seek out ways to improve and is not able to pass judgment on the quality of any given material. He does not experience envy, greed, or the drive to be the best. He is comfortable with himself and does not approach life seeking to place value on the things around him. He simply accepts, unconditionally, that all things are equal, and he only desires the basic necessities of his world. His is not a world of external values, values artificially placed by human beings as they manipulate the economic system; he values the lives around him. Rather than place a monetary value on all he sees, Joel, instead, values people and life.

Try taking a day to see the world through the eyes of the egalitarian Joel. All becomes tinted; all becomes equal, and, most importantly, all becomes beautiful.

Twenty-One

Lack of Reality

One day, Joel, who was in a talking mood and was sharing many of his thoughts and ideas, began planning his future. He mentioned playing the organ in a church, perhaps going to school, working in a library, and having a family. We have heard these thoughts before and always try to offer support, but we also try to steer him in positive directions. But as he talked about having a family and wanting three children (Sometimes it is six!), he blurted out that he didn't want them to be like him, that his children would be "normal".

We were shocked to hear that sentiment from him and were not sure how to respond. With a typical human response of avoidance, we changed the subject and went on to discuss less potentially excrescent topics, such as what was for dinner. But the comment remained with me all week. In a rare moment of lucidity, Joel had expressed a deep fear and self-awareness. I decided to think more on this problem and be more sensitive to his self-esteem.

He is aware of his limitations and does not always like the fact that he is unable to do the things other people can do. He would like to go to college, get a degree, get married, and have children, but deep down he suspects that those opportunities are not in the blueprint for his life. Because reality is not the preferred thinking mode, he often resides in a state of unreality, governed by television shows or places he has seen or heard about. He avoids comparing himself to his brothers with the awareness that he is different. He wants to live an 'ordinary' life, but in some ways, he would like to design 'ordinary' for himself rather than have others design it for him.

Perhaps deep down he does struggle with self-esteem, with insecurity, with a lack of confidence, but in many ways he also seems satisfied with himself and comfortable in his own skin. Should parents expend energy teaching their autistic child to accept his or her limitations, or is there strength in teaching the child that nothing is outside their capabilities? Is there an appropriate balance between encouraging dreams and recognizing realities? We have always sought the right balance for Joel, but we have never been sure if we have found it. I suppose that only time will tell.

Parents everywhere wonder what their children will become, what their abilities are, or where their interests lie. These worries are more paramount for the parents of autistic children. The famous song "*Que Sera, Sera*" that Doris Day sang so beautifully may be warm and charming to most parents, but, unfortunately, the parents of autistic children do not have the luxury of subscribing to its tenets.

We knew Joel had certain gifts at a young age, but we could not decide if those gifts were merely interests or special abilities. Nevertheless, it was apparent that he had a thorough understanding and keen interest in the alphabet. Looking back, it should have been obvious that his abilities to sort in alphabetical order and memorize words and systems accordingly were his destiny for his career.

It began with saying the alphabet forward and backward, followed by the ability to number the alphabet and identify the letter from its ordered number. This led to an exceptional ability to spell words and identify words that were misspelled. Although successful at times, Joel did not always win spelling contests, partly due to his hesitancy to vocalize the correct spelling of the word and partly due to his not being able to operate within time constraints. That stated, his spelling prowess was and is simply an extension of his knowledge of the alphabet and how words are put together.

It was then logical that Joel would eventually end up in a library shelving books, which is what he does every afternoon. While we have little firsthand knowledge of his competency, neither have we heard any complaints. According to Joel, he puts away between 40 and 100 books each day, and he has never made a mistake. He further states that he knows every book in the library and can find any book that is requested. This makes his gifts extraordinary in some ways and invaluable to a library. It oddly renders a card catalog, particularly the title section, relatively ineffective as a distinguishing system for finding a book.

Yet, in spite of these unusual abilities, Joel does not seem to apply joyful emotion to his experience nor his competency. While most people would express pride at their ability to sort books and memorize a library, Joel approaches this skill with the same objectivity of most events. His emotion is stoic, neither joyful nor sad, neither prideful nor humble, it is simply factual without expressive intent. In spite of this seeming indifference, he is excellent at his job, and for that we are grateful. We are fortunate to have found a skill for Joel that is both useful and unusual.

Twenty-Two

The Economics of Education

The students wore ties; the faculty members were moved, and there was a general outpouring of love and support for Joel as he concluded his last day of school. While to Joel it might have seemed unusual, and I have little doubt that he never understood what the tears were all about, nevertheless, he was aware that he was being honored. While he may have been confused by all the attention, he also responded with hugs and sincere appreciation. But why all the fuss? Isn't Joel simply one of thousands of students who graduate from high school?

The show of warm affection mingled sweetly and nostalgically with the sadness, as the students and faculty gathered around Joel to demonstrate what he has meant to them through the years. Joel's disability, autism, mixed with learning problems, could have resulted in rejection, loneliness, and alienation, as he did his best to fit in with a public school system whose prime concern is to meet or exceed academic expectations on standardized examinations. Instead, his disability somehow resulted in unconditional acceptance. Never mentioned, but maybe foremost in an administrator's mind, has to be the cost of educating a student so different from the model needed for institutional success. Joel, in his thirteen school years, cost the district time, money, and, to a small degree, academic reputation. Not only that, there is the peripheral curiosity that the time Joel required may have taken away from other children's educational needs. His need for specialized classes, teacher's aides, almost constant attention, modified grades, meetings, individualized teaching, and unique scheduling, had to have been a serious drain on the resources of the district.

But, ironically, the cost of educating Joel was much less than the gain. Economically, when I spend money on an item, I hope to gain more than I spend, whether it is a car, computer, clothes, or food. If I buy something that quickly breaks, then I realize I spent more than I gained. Yet if the car I purchased helps me make a living, then it is my contention that I have gained more than I lost (unless, of course, fuel and upkeep costs keep escalating!). Obviously, people are worth the investment and should not be considered objects or commodities for consumer consumption. Yet, even from an economic standpoint, is it possible that Joel was worth more than he cost? I believe the answer is—yes.

The surface explanation is that any cost that leads to the education of a child to make him a productive, contributing member of society is beneficial to the common good. And, no doubt, in spite of his disability, Joel's education has helped him to cope, to adjust, to think critically, and to make his own decisions, at least to an extent. The relentless commitment to Joel's improvement, the concerted effort of teachers, other students, administration, and, yes, even custodians and maintenance workers, all came together in a glorious chorus of dedication to helping a disabled child.

But returning to the question: What did they gain? Why invest so much effort into one person? Were they simply doing their jobs, or was there more to it? As I watched the myriad of reactions to Joel's departure from school, I realized, not for the first time, that it was not Joel who was being honored, but, rather, it was Joel who had done the honoring for the last thirteen years. Joel was simply being thanked, thanked for all he had done for everyone else.

He was being thanked for the smiles, the handshakes, the hugs, the encouragement, the support for everyone . . . for everything, thanked for the consistently good attitude, the effort, the adherence to looking his best, the absence of ugliness, bad language, and unkind words. He was thanked for being true to himself without malice, without pretensions, and without the lies that often accompany students trying to make themselves look better. He was thanked for his unceasing and transparent honesty. *He* was thanked for making *their* world a better place. His value was and is immeasurable, and in economic terms, the demand for Joel is far greater than the supply.

Tip:

Education is what it is all about in autism, but not in the traditional model. Because the autistic thinks differently and sees the world uniquely, teaching requires a different approach. Just remember to keep the routines, use pictures, be deliberate, and avoid subtleties. Help schools and teachers understand the disability.

Twenty-Three

The Cell Phone

It was with some reservation and curiosity that we finally purchased a cell phone for Joel. Our reservations were primarily based on whether or not he was able to manipulate the sequence and order required to make and answer calls, to set up contacts, and to send text messages, plus the responsibility of keeping up with it. But the need to have ease of communication, knowing where he is, and giving him a sense of security, all added up to his having a cell phone. I went to the cell phone store to pick one out with the typical concerns of price, size, style, color, screen, and all those things that make each phone unique. After a confusing thirty minutes of a salesman explaining the differences, I landed on a little flip phone with a choice of red, black, or blue. Settling on the blue one and picking the contract system for the next year, I took it home, gift-wrapped it (Okay, my wife actually wrapped it.), and placed it under the tree.

Christmas morning, he opened it up, and with his typical stoic reaction, he said, "Thank you," and proceeded to some other gifts. After all was done, I turned to Joel and asked him if he liked his new cell phone. He, of course, said yes, and in his customary, understated manner, he mentioned that he liked all his gifts equally and was glad it was Christmas. I knew I would need to show him some things about the phone, but I wasn't entirely sure how to go about teaching him the basics. Luckily, his younger brother, a precociously gifted and compassionate child, decided to take it on himself to teach Joel. Remember that virtually every behavior and action must be taught to autistics. This is due to their lack of perception of social behavior and their general lack of creative curiosity. In addition, while they enjoy new things, they usually do not have an innate desire to explore and discover, or, at least, they usually do not have the knowledge needed for such endeavors.

But Joel's brother, Jordan, jumped in and created family contacts. Plus, a few friends taught him how to answer the phone and how to send a text message. I then showed Joel how to place the phone in the holster and how to attach it to the belt. He now walks around with his phone on his side, wearing a tie, and a slight swagger, with a kind of pride demonstrating that he has arrived in the world! When we call him or send him a message, he is a bit slow at responding, but in his cautious way he does get the job done.

I realize now that given the right instructions, the right circumstances, and, mostly, a great deal of patience, Joel can learn how to navigate through a cell phone. I also recognize how much security this gives him and mostly gives us, as we prepare him for the working world. If he will keep it with him, we will always know where he is and how he is doing. At the same time, it is also our continued goal and responsibility to help him to be as independent as possible and to make his own decisions. The cell phone is an ideal way for us to monitor his activities a little, yet give him room to make his own mistakes and his own successes. But we are only a call away from helping him if he is in a predicament, or lost, or frightened. Obviously, more teaching of when to use it is needed, but, in general, my comfort level about this new item for Joel is quite high. Does his having a cell phone increase our responsibility? Absolutely. His awareness of the ability to contact anyone at anytime requires us to teach him whom to contact and when, for without that level of knowledge, Joel may fall into the mistake of assuming that everyone is waiting for him to call them.

I believe that autistic adults need and deserve a cell phone, but they also need careful teaching on appropriate usage. Mostly, autistic adults and children must have someone or many someones who love and care about them. Sometimes loving and caring takes the form of allowing effort and encouraging independence.

After thinking about autism and cell phones and writing down a few thoughts on the subject, I discovered that the same title had been used for an entirely different purpose. To that end, I am writing a follow-up, addressing the same topic but for a new reason, the reason being that I do not believe that cell phones are causing a rise in autism in our culture. As proposed by many, the argument in favor of such posturing is that cases of autism increased at approximately the same rate and at the same time we saw a rise in cell phone usage.

I am not a scientist and have little to substantiate my beliefs other than years of studying findings plus many years of searching for causes as well as cures for autism. We have examined pollutants, allergies, enzymes, food, weather, animals, vitamins, minerals, water, medicines, and homeopathy, and we have experimented with all the known forms of cures that are within our limited budget. Obviously, there are other cures outside of our resources that we are still considering. Yet, with the thousands of suggestions for causes and cures, and much research, and devotion to the problem, and absolute commitment to finding a cure, much of, but not all of autism remains a mystery.

Not that I am suggesting we give up. No! In fact, I continue to hope and pray for the magic dust that will fix all of the problems with autism and autistic students. Some of the mystery, indeed, involves the proliferation of autism, or at least the identification of children with that particular disability over the last ten years, matching that of the rise of the cell phone. During the last ten years, we have also seen the decline of base stealing in baseball, an awareness of steroid use in sports, the rise of the mp3 player, an increase in Starbucks coffee houses, an increase in body piercings, the stunning success of Google, and the spectacular popularity of teen idol Justin Bieber. All this is to say that any extended period of time usually demonstrates a marked ebb and flow of ideas, people, objects, inventions, events, and circumstances. It is possible, and in some cases likely, that such growth in one is related to or even causes another, or that a decline leads to a rise in something else. Because correlation does not equal causation, it is also likely that the events are totally unrelated.

I have no irrefutable proof for what I believe, and only time with careful data will determine the truth, but for now I will stand firm that cell phones are not causing autism, and for people to think such a thing detracts from where the truth will be found. The truth to the causes and cure for autism will be found in the DNA, from the millions of strands being studied at this very moment, in the thousands of laboratories across the country, by the scientists and mathematicians looking for the abnormality we know as autism. Meanwhile, parents and physicians continue to try different approaches to help—and virtually every technique is beneficial.

Good nutrition, vitamins, breathing, therapy, behavior techniques, more sleep, order, quiet, organization, and deliberation are all appropriate and productive in helping the autistic. No doubt, allergies, pollutants, stress, disease, and various other problems have contributed to the increase in autism. Yet there is also no doubt that we are identifying the disability, which has become quite broad in scope, earlier and more accurately, in an effort to help these children adapt better in an educational environment.

Back to our issue: Is it possible that cell phones, with their electromagnetic radiation, have added to the rise of autism? I suppose it is possible. Is it likely? I think not. Meanwhile, let's continue to help the disabled, and let's continue to search for a cure. Until that time occurs, however, we should avoid blaming outside sources for this problem and focus our attention on improvement, on education, and on coping skills.

Twenty-Four

Autism and Homework

N ow that school is over for our autistic son, I would like to give some helpful hints to parents and teachers about ideas to help the educational process.

Tip:

If a worksheet has misspelled words, poor copy quality (blurry), or even words cut off the edge or bottom, it will be such a distraction to the autistic student that he will not be able to focus on the content. In the same manner, an autistic person cannot filter unimportant sounds—it may seem he is ignoring or not hearing instructions, but he hears them along with the hum of the air conditioner, outside talking, lawn mowers, etc. That is why they are such visual learners and need written or picture instructions.

Homework that is assigned to students will always be a controversial topic in education, especially given the schedules that many students keep after school. But also the pressure to keep standardized test scores at a high rating causes schools to remain committed to constant improvement. A certain degree of homework can supplement the in-school process, or, in the case of students unable to complete assigned work during the day, homework can keep slower students from falling behind. It can also be a great burden to both the student and the parents. When homework causes serious emotional distress and becomes a time-consuming project to the exclusion of family time, personal endeavors, or positive support, then the gain is actually a loss—a bear market with little hope for a rebound. This is often the case with autistic students.

For us and for Joel, a synonym for homework ought to be "home torture" due to the pain and suffering we all experienced. Tears, stress, worry, and headaches accompanied the efforts to get Joel to get his work done. Home was not a time for schoolwork . . . in his mind. School was for schoolwork, and home was for other things. To mix the two was to break the routine, a decidedly difficult event for autistic children.

Autism is a difficult disability to define, partly due to its complexity and diversity, and partly due to the often accompanying disabilities such as speech problems, reading disorders, behavior problems, and various learning challenges. Since these problems may or may not attend during the day, it should come as no surprise when a teacher assigns work to be done at home, assuming the student would benefit from the supplemental learning experience or stay caught up on the work required. But, sadly, unless the instructions are very explicit, and unless the required work is prepared to accommodate the disability, most likely the homework will take several hours and be a combined effort, or combined torture, of student and parent.

Educating the autistic, as has been discussed in earlier chapters, requires a thorough and precise process, to include modeling, pictures, limited sequencing, and opportunities for practice. While homework can include these elements, most likely, unless the teacher has provided some of this, and unless the parent has received the proper training, the homework will be missing some of these necessary ingredients for success, making it a hardship for everyone and most likely a moving target for any kind of winning benefit. This probably becomes compounded as the autistic student progresses through the grade levels and has several different teachers and several different subjects, all of whom are committed to the finest in education for all students. It then becomes a difficult arena for even the most advanced student to deal with five or six different homework expectations, with the difficulty multiplied several times for the autistic student and his parents.

So how do we solve this problem? We do not necessarily advocate zero homework, for there is no question that study time and supplemental work can be constructive when handled judiciously. And we certainly do not advocate lower expectations in the classroom, for many autistic students can learn at, or sometimes beyond, the level of other students. But the system has to be different from the norm, with great preparation and exact deliberation of presentation, allowing for time, minimal distractions, and fewer problems on each page. Mostly, it is necessary to provide a thorough education to teachers and parents that will prevent any kind of stressful home situation, including excess homework time, emotional strain, and negative educational dividends.

To teachers, I suggest coordinating the homework assignments with the other teachers to prevent too many subjects being dealt with at home. This may require a bit of centralization through the system, but it is definitely worth the challenge. I also recommend that when homework is necessary, the teacher give very specific instructions as to the expectation, including minor recommendations, such as pencil or pen or time suggestions. Furthermore, make sure that no homework assignment would take more than thirty minutes.

Remember a rule of thumb of doubling the time: a thirty-minute assignment will probably take an autistic student sixty minutes.

To the parent, I suggest that you don't allow the total homework to exceed sixty minutes, and thirty minutes is much preferred. Avoid any kind of emotional duress or excess tension during the process. Help your child to think critically by encouraging the responses rather than providing the answers for him. Remember that our goal is independence, with the ability to make informed, responsible decisions. Mostly, remain committed to the educational process, knowing that teachers and schools have the best interest of the student at heart, but also be firm in your convictions to develop a healthy, loving, and patient environment both at school and at home.

Tip:

For older high-functioning students (4th or 5th grade on up), the use of an assignment card is very effective. Write or type on a small piece of tag board these four questions, leaving space to write with a dry erase marker:

1. What is my assignment?
2. How much/many do I need to finish?
3. How long do I have to do this?
4. What do I do when I've finished?

Laminate the card so it can be re-used, and then velcro or attach it to the student's work space. If the student seems off task, point to or remind him of the instructions on the card.

Twenty-Five

Deciphering the Social Contract

Most people respond in communication to events around us, perceiving situations, whether due to social activities or physical properties, that, in turn, give us the message of what to do, what to say, or how to react. This type of behavior happens unconsciously and naturally all the time and is actually the result of years of awareness of our surroundings. It is the process of what is referred to as 'contractarianism', an unwritten contract between people which allows the give and take of conversation and communication. Of course, we have all committed that inevitable and often disturbing social blunder; saying the wrong thing at the wrong time, using the wrong fork, or perhaps wearing the wrong clothes, but, in general, we work to retain individuality while fitting in with our environment. When we understand what is happening around us, we are able to belong, while having influence at the same time.

In addition, our natural survival instincts warn us and teach us how to react to stimuli presented almost daily. Sudden or unusual sounds, motions, and feelings all dictate our immediate behavior, at least to an extent, giving us a constant awareness and perception of danger or of comfort. One night, as I was driving home from a nearby city, going sixty-five miles per hour, I suddenly happened upon a large deer in my path. Logic reminded me to hit the deer (at least this is the recommendation by some, due to the fear of rolling over) and face the consequences, but my survival instinct told me to swerve in avoidance. Luckily, the same instinct told me to correct my swerve a little but not too suddenly, and within seconds, I was on my way, having missed the deer by a foot or two. I had perceived a dangerous situation, altered my circumstances, fixed the problem, and rejoiced in relief that the danger was passed.

Joel does not enjoy those same survival instincts. He either does not have the reaction time to make decisions, or, more likely, he does not perceive his environment in the same way that other people do. If he were to drive, he probably would have hit the deer. Joel's disability does not permit him to have a realistic awareness of the world around him. This includes traffic problems or complex emotions; even the passing of time can be a mystery to Joel. While he is peripherally aware of anger, tension, or problems that may exist, those things are generally abstract and do not directly affect him. It makes for a rose-tinted world, a world where everyone and everything is a friend, a world of no "sorrows or dangers or toils or snares". This is a form of extreme sheltering that is natural and inherent rather than imposed or taught by others. While he would never say it, it is not unlike the statement, "I am sheltered and self-protected by my own inability to know reality; this makes me happy."

This is the cause of two circumstances: 1) A young adult enters the world contented and happy due to being unaware of the challenges facing him, and 2) Caregivers are very concerned about his future and how to give him a degree of independence while insuring his safety. But the hard truth is that Joel is going to have to enter the world unprepared, at least to an extent, through no fault of his own or of anyone else, for its harsh realities. This requires that others become sensitive, compassionate, helpful, and forthright.

Returning to the purpose of these chapters, I am encouraging employers, drivers, clients, students, and all those who encounter Joel (or the other Joels of this world), to give him a chance to be successful, to encourage him, to guide him, to help him, to be firm when needed, to love him, and, mostly, to allow him to fit in. He, like everyone else, deserves a chance and an opportunity to give it a try. While we are not so naive as to believe that he will be successful at everything, and we are certainly aware of his limitations, we are also convinced that through cooperation, patience, and training that there is a place for Joel in this world. So, I ask that we build a hedge of protection around him, but that within that hedge we push him to greater heights which will actually allow him to reach his potential. And as you afford him the opportunity and give him a chance to try, watch out for him along the way. It's going to take the concerted effort of many people for him to be safe and to succeed.

With Joel completing his high school years, it became paramount for his guardians to provide for his well-being and give him the opportunity for meaning in his life. Yet many questions remained with us as his guardians, of our role, our goals for him, his preferences, and our community's acceptance of his differences. Should he try to get a job? If so, what kind of job? Should he stay at home? If so, what would he do? He watches television; he plays some games on the computer, but he doesn't read much; he doesn't get much physical activity. What would he do?

Connected to these concerns were even more basic questions. What and where would he eat? How would he go places? Would he take care of himself without our constant prompting? Could he handle people's questions, or would he be assertive enough to solve his own life problems? Simple things such as bathrooms, drinking fountains, grooming, blowing his nose, and all the things that we take for granted have to be taught to Joel. For us, the easiest thing would be to leave him home with lots of food in the

109

pantry and not worry about it. But the question remains; what is best for Joel?

So we entered the rushing, turbulent river of life with great care and not just a little trepidation, looking for the calmest spot with shallow water, stepping gingerly so as not to fall or upset the current flow too much. We held his hand, knowing that we would need to let go when we were sure his feet and his journey would take him across. We then watched, ready to grab him if needed, ready to steady his steps, ready to find another crossing spot, but also ready to let him do this by himself.

It was all a careful and deliberate process of preparation and education for him and for us. Step one: Find out Joel's goals, and make sure that they are consistent with our own goals for him. Step Two: Find territory to match his goals. Step Three: Contact City Rides for scheduling and transportation possibilities. Step Four: Educate Joel on the process. Step Five: Monitor him closely but encourage independence.

Joel's goals were to work in a library shelving and sorting books and to work in the mail room at the local university sorting mail and delivering packages. He also did not want to wake up too early for this, but did want some time to practice organ at school, if possible. Thankfully, and not surprising, these goals matched our own. Finding the territory was a little difficult and involved interviewing librarians and mailroom workers. The interview also gave prospective employers an education and an opportunity to meet Joel and to learn how to deal with him. Again, thankfully, we found employers willing to give it a try. In my mind, these are the heroes of this story . . . people willing to take a risk to help a disabled adult.

The transportation part of this story was complicated at first, due to our living away from the city and our concern about Joel's readiness to get on a bus by himself. Yet, for minimal cost, a small bus pulls up to our house, and Joel gets on the bus to ride to work every day at 12:30. It is a remarkably efficient system with drivers who care and make safety and comfort a priority.

We spent two days doing a dry run with Joel and showing him the path and the system for success. He was both malleable and excited about the opportunity. We then double-checked with the people to make sure all was in place before starting. For the first few days we monitored the process, made a couple of adjustments, and then let Joel do it on his own.

While we are not so naive as to believe that all is perfect, at this point it is working much better than expected. He has risen to the challenge, has responded with independence, and feels like he is a contributing member of society. While he is not yet a paid employee, since all is voluntary, we are hoping to move him into these same positions as a part-time paid employee. Part of the reason he is not being paid at this point is the restrictive minimum wage law that does not allow employers to pay less. I have good reason to suspect that the employers would be more willing to pay him something if they did not have to pay minimum wage. This is an example of how minimum wage hurts, not helps, the disabled. Meanwhile, we and Joel are excited with his success, a success that was not anticipated but is much appreciated.

Tip:

Work to find a useful and meaningful skill which serves a functional purpose but is also unique to the individual. It could be proofreading, food related, growing things, or computer skills. All these and more help an autistic adult fit into the world.

Twenty-Six

Black and White

Driving down the street, on our way to get a treat at Sonic, Joel and I began talking about sonic booms. I reminisced about my childhood when I heard jet airplanes overhead break the sound barrier resulting in a resonant bass sound that caused the windows to shake and the dishes to rattle. As a small child it was rather frightening, but when my dad explained the cause, it became rather exhilarating to imagine the speed of the jet that could move faster than sound.

While explaining to Joel about sonic booms, I moved into my "cliché" mode of talking, where I began a repetitive series of quasi-complaints about modern culture. It is my own ironic brand of making fun of people who want to return to the "good old days". When I get going, it can be quite entertaining and absolutely harmless, with shades of sarcasm and irony thrown in for the sheer joy of the moment. So I was pontificating about the days when girls didn't call boys on the phone, when you didn't have to pump your own gas, when there was only one kind of coffee, and when there were very few radio stations. I moved into television and began talking about the days of antennae on the TV and having to watch everything in black and white.

Suddenly, although he had been silent for quite a while (a normal response to my routine!), he asked me a question, "Dad, was everything in black and white in the good old days?" I said,

"Yes, Joel, we didn't get a color television until I was older." He said, "No, I mean was *everything* in black and white?"

I sat stunned for a minute, as I thought through his question, *Is his perspective of the world based on television? If all on the television were black and white, did that make the world black and white as well? Does he not understand the development of science and technology and that television is a reflection of advancing technology? Or was the question actually latently perceptive? Has the growth and hyper-charge of technology actually colored our world? Were we figuratively and collectively more "black and white" many years ago?*

Our world is complicated by choice, by color, and by a blending and amalgamation of styles, cultures, values, concepts, interests, and preferences. Having choices is part of the joy of our world and part of the excitement of living. The entertainment world seems to be a manifestation of the complexity and color that we live with each and every day. This makes our perception of reality to be both confusing and ever-changing . . . a sort of wonderland or even Disneyland of options.

Yet, for Joel, perhaps he would prefer less choices, fewer options. Perhaps his world is black and white, and, maybe, in some ways, he is better off with his perception. I like the choices; I like the color; I like the complexity, but it sure can make for a lot of decisions.

Twenty-Seven

Eradication of the Cherry

While walking through the mall, casually shopping for clothes and looking in the various stores along the path, Joel mentioned that he would like to get a Coke at Chick-fil-A. Gladly accommodating his request, we ambled in that direction, entered the fast-food restaurant, walked up to the counter, and stood in line to order our drinks. Jacob had mentioned that he wouldn't mind having a cup of lemonade as well. But the poster of the new Peppermint Strawberry Shake caught Joel's attention.

His eyes shone brightly as he changed his mind, and he asked me about getting the shake rather than the Coke. I said sure, no problem, and he then said the words, "But no cherry." Being in an agreeable mood, I said, "Yes," rather absently and stood in line to order our drinks. Standing in any line is a challenge for me, not being of patient spirit. To pass the time, I can be found reading, looking around, thinking hard, imagining a world without lines, or performing a plethora of mental activities. In this case, I simply visited another cognitive zone for a few minutes. Finally I ordered the drinks, forgetting, unfortunately, to ask for the cherry to be excluded.

After receiving the drinks, we left the mall to head for the truck with the goal of driving home. On the way, Joel, in his objective but pointed manner, mentioned that the cherry was in the shake. Not necessarily accusingly or forgivingly, he pointed out that he did not want the cherry. Climbing into the truck, Joel tried in vain to get the cherry out. Refusing to drink the shake with the cherry, he had inadvertently engorged the dastardly object further down into the shake in his efforts to rid the refreshment of the ugliness known as a cherry.

Knowing he would not drink the shake until the cherry was gone, I asked Jacob to help him. Jacob did so, and together they dug into the shake, found the cherry, and removed the obstacle, which Jacob subsequently ate in great haste to encourage Joel to drink his Peppermint Strawberry Shake! All was well and Joel was happy.

Joel's autism does have an odd and often debilitating result; he gets focused on something and cannot let it go, regardless of the seemingly innocuousness of the situation. To us it is just a little cherry in the midst of something wonderful, but to Joel it is the central block to enjoyment. Take the problem away . . . and happiness ensues. Our job as parents is to discern and predict the potential enemy before it enters the scene.

Tip:

Quirks and eccentricities are traits of autism. Autistics tend to latch onto particular clothes, food, systems, ideas, and routines that are difficult to change. It makes the person rather odd and unusual to other people, but to him, it all feels normal.

Twenty-Eight

Texting vs Speaking

Joel has difficulty speaking most of the time. On some days, he speaks little to none, while, at other times, he is a little more verbose. Yet, even in his talking moments, rarely does he have something substantial to say. On good days, he is full of questions that seem to build on each other. The questions could be about family members, what hymns we are singing, the starting times of events, how old people are, or what instruments are being used. Mainly, though, spoken language is a challenge for Joel, and he mostly finds himself nodding or speaking very quietly.

Yet, a new and rather stunning development has occurred. Joel enjoys texting on his phone. He writes long involved texts that demonstrate a deeper understanding of life, a way to seek beyond the obvious, and a way to express his emotions. Below are some of his texts:

'Hey daddy can you pick me up around 4:00 so I can get my haircut afterwards? See you in an hour and forty-five minutes! Do you think it is going to snow tonight? It is kind of chilly outside! Brrrr! I am taking a cold rc cola break at the library! I am dressed kind of warm! I have a scarf some gloves a hat a jacket and a sweater! Are you wearing a tie today or a turtle neck? I am going to shelve some more books here in a minute! Then I will call you at around 4:00 to pick me up in time to take me to get a haircut!

Ttyl bye! P.S. It is my birthday in 5 days! I am going to be 20 years old! Yay!'

'Thanks dad! Do you mind if I wait outside for you at around 3:30? I shelved lots of books today at the library and I might shelve some more books here in just a few minutes! See you at 3:45! Tell all the professors of Howard Payne University I said hi and tell all the students I said hi too! Ttyl bye!'

Of course some texts are shorter and simpler, but, in general, he speaks more through texting than through talking. Why is this? Is it the strange block that occurs from the brain to the mouth for some autistic children? Does texting actually allow a circumventing of the neurons needed for speaking? Perhaps communication for an autistic child is deeper, requiring a different form and transit from which we are familiar. Perhaps the conduit for expression is a channel not usually found in most people.

Whatever the reason, we are enjoying the new communication, and we are enjoying discovering a personality that shines forth from the cell phone! Ah, Joel . . . always keeps us on our toes.

Twenty-Nine

Time: A Constant Mystery

The passing of time as we understand it is an arbitrary and artificially applied concept, humanly divined and codified for selfish purposes. Our lives are ordered by time, and we are dependent upon the system we have established for ourselves, a system that is both frustrating and liberating. Nevertheless, regardless of the historical development of how time moves, with its expression of the rotation of the Earth, the Sun, the changing seasons, the pull of gravity, and the complexity of relativity of space and matter, we are obligated to operate within the established code of time, which may be naturally driven or socially constrained by culture.

Do we eat three meals a day, morning, noon, and evening, because our bodies tell us to do so? Or have we fallen into this concept by virtue of the design of our lives, thus forcing our bodies into a fallacy of the need for three meals equally spaced? Do we sleep at night because it is dark or because of the physical requirement for rest—or perhaps because of a combination of both? Our watches and clocks remind us of the time, which, in turn, sends a message of an upcoming event or obligation. Schools, businesses, institutions, travel, energy—all depend on our system of time and our understanding of its movement and passage.

Yet, for Joel, time has no meaning. He does not understand nor embrace in any sense the passing of time. For him, time stands still, and he almost resents having to conform to the system that

119

has been codified and efficaciously applied. He recognizes the actions of a clock and is frequently reminded of seconds, minutes, and hours, but those odd increments are but words to be used when confounded by forthcoming events. The concept of time spent on an activity has no meaning, and the word 'hurry' is not a part of his vocabulary.

This makes Joel's existence rather random yet also ironically regimented. Because the passing of time is essentially a mystery, he must apply rigor, ritual, and routine to everything that he does. The more routine, the more successful he will become. Yet surrounding that routine and enveloping the action is the overriding lack of concern about length or expectations. This makes for a tension-filled universe for everyone else connected to Joel, but not for him. His contentment with time playing little to no role in his life is wildly frustrating for others but wildly comforting for him.

For the autistic child, his inner peace is found in the personal expression of his interests, focusing on those activities for which he is successful, regardless of their niche in the world. I knew one autistic child who constantly drew maps of the world. Sometimes the maps were detailed and at other times rather general. The maps served no real purpose, since better maps are attainable at any bookstore, yet he continued to draw maps as a way to fulfill his own peculiar brand of self-expression.

Joel finds satisfaction in playing the piano and the organ, as well as listening to classical music or watching certain television shows. While none of these activities serve a great market need in the world, and riches are most likely not going to occur from his interests, nevertheless, he does express his joy through these events. An autistic child is not seeking to find his place in the world, rather, he has already found it and is comfortable in that residence. For Joel, the passing of time is some kind of mysterious force that plays little to no role in his theater, a theater that consists of his own designs for expression.

Yet, truthfully, the world cannot operate singularly and one-dimensionally. Monody is charming and refreshing but cannot compete with the beauties and complexities of polyphony. Joel's rejection of time is one of his many endearing qualities that make him who he is, but it also prevents him from collective congruency in social interaction. We are a time-mandated culture, and operating outside of the time boundary is anathema in today's world.

This makes for a pleasant tension, as we continually teach Joel the meaning of time, which he artfully rejects. It remains a mystery to him!

Joel has almost no concept of time. His time responses are simply physiological rather than dictated by any kind of external restraints. Yes, he carries a watch and occasionally glances at it for some kind of general idea, but he makes few if any decisions based on the passage of time. When we name a specific time for an event, he does consider it in his planning, but simply in the way that the event and time match each other. The passing of time leading to that designated event has no merit in his thinking. Time remains a mystery to Joel.

In some ways, however, there is joy in the emancipation from the passing of time. Imagine a world without clocks, without deadlines, without appointments, or without specific time requirements. Imagine eating, sleeping, talking, going, or doing things whenever you felt like it. What kind of strange and marvelous existence would it be to have no awareness of the clock, the watch, or the timekeeper? What if you never dealt with your own impatience or the impatience of someone else? What if the task had no deadline, and you could deal with it at your leisure? Would this make your life all about leisure and pleasure? This is the natural world of Joel.

Yet, it is an artificial world and one that has no bearing on the "real" world in which we reside. While we could quibble about the human imposition of time on our lives, in truth—it is a reality.

We have to follow society's time schedule, and so must Joel. Here is where the intersection of autism and reality clash without any kind of ideal resolution. Society's insistence on following a time schedule and Joel's natural predilection for not knowing that time is passing makes for an incongruent and nearly impossible situation.

As parents, though, we do not give up and accept Joel's lack of time awareness. Doing so would make Joel even less contributing and without meaning in today's world. Instead, we constantly remind him of the passing of time, remind him to study the clock, and we remind him to reference the upcoming events. We mention how long something will take, to point out that we must not forget or ignore the clock as it steadily moves.

And, in some intangible way, Joel's lack of the concept of time is related to his general sluggishness, lack of preparation, and very little progressive thinking. His life-responses then are rather random and undetermined by any outside force, with little regard to the things that must get done. Most people wake up and give thought to the passing of time and how the goals of the day need to be met—Joel does not think about any of those things.

In the end, however, Joel is probably happier for not having constant time considerations. We are not happy with him in this regard, in that he does not and cannot fit into our schedule, but he does find joy in the lack of constraints. Keep in mind, however, that Joel does not actively resist time; he simply has no consideration for it, not out of rebellion, but more out of a lack of awareness. He is blissfully content not to be aware of time, but we are continually wishing for him to know time and to live closer to the clock. It makes for constant frustration for us, but it makes no difference to him.

Thirty

Clothes

Joel has always been caught up in clothes and particularly the value of matching. He prefers that his clothes match and that his ensemble presentation is of high quality. This is in contrast to the personal appearance of his face, hair, and teeth. We do not understand the disparity in the concepts, but there is no doubt that he has high standards with regard to clothing and low standards with regard to his personal hygiene and appearance.

Sometimes as early as three days away from Sunday, he will pick out his clothes and place them aside. This could include a shirt, matching tie, pants, and coat, with an added sweater during the winter months. Recently, he asked me if he could pick out his clothes for Sunday. I said, "Sure," but I asked him what he was thinking about. He looked at me quizzically, so I altered my question:

Dad: "Joel, what are you imagining that you will wear to church?"
Joel: (with a perplexed face): "Clothes."
Dad: "What color of clothes?"
Joel: "Matching."
Dad: "Anything specific in mind?"
Joel: "Nice clothes."
Dad: "What kind of nice clothes?"
Joel: "Church clothes."

Joel's lack of imagination is extended to virtually all activities in life, resulting in a lack of conceptual thinking and an establishment of certain expectations. His approach to determining the best clothes or what to eat is broad and conceived more from experience than from specifically imagined details. Rather than visualizing himself in particular clothes to look a certain way, and then finding clothes to match the visualization, he, instead, has a general idea in his mind of what to expect, and then he seeks the object to meet those broad expectations.

His lack of imagination is directly related to his limited creativity. Although he is primarily a visual learner, visualization in the mind is a creative project rooted in and formed by the imagination. This is true for everyone. Using creativity, we design a picture in our mind, which then becomes our imagination, which leads to a concrete picture forming a concept of the item or event. If creativity is limited, so goes the imagination. If the imagination is limited, so goes the concept. Without a concept, we are dependent on the concrete items for the design.

Such is the case with Joel. In his mind, he has the broad sense of what he needs, but he requires the use of the other senses to determine the final product. When I asked him what clothes he wanted to wear, his concept was generally correct but without specifics. He had to see the clothes before deciding what exactly to wear. His concept is formed after experiencing the concrete—and not before. Joel's decision-making abilities are based on what he knows, sees, and touches, so it becomes necessary for us to remember this as we help him adjust to life.

Use visuals such as pictures in a sequence to teach or remind the child of certain procedures. Pictures of getting ready for school, doing chores/homework, or getting ready for bed are helpful for non-readers.

Thirty-One

Communication

His voice is too soft; he has trouble looking people in the eyes, and it is difficult to have meaningful or creative conversations. He is able to answer questions, respond using short answers, nod, smile, and can use his body to reflect the nature of the conversation. Yet when responses begin to require creativity, use picturesque language, or take a deeper approach, he tends to shut the mental door and seeks to escape the situation.

The problems of communication are compounded by Joel's tendency to believe that others are thinking the same thoughts he is thinking. When asked what he thinks other people are thinking, he responds with his own thoughts rather than working to perceiving what others might be thinking. Connected to this problem is his inability to understand facial expressions and respond according to what he sees. Not being able to recognizing bad moods, anger, or fear in other people, he assumes that everyone is happy and thinking what he thinks. This then causes verbal communication to be redundant and unnecessary.

The talking softly is a little harder to explain, since he seems to enjoy playing the piano and the organ at extreme volumes. Somehow, though, it is related to expressing what is inside him. Since it is basically unnecessary, due to other people thinking what he thinks, it is not important to speak loud enough for others to hear. Unfortunately, this means that those who are hearing-impaired or simply a little hard of hearing assume that Joel simply does not speak. They cannot hear him; he doesn't move his mouth very much, so he does not communicate. Since the expectation is for him not to speak, and human beings generally fulfill the level of expectations set forth, Joel responds by talking less.

Yet communication can take many forms, including cell phones and body language, both of which he practices to great success. He enjoys texting on his phone, and time has shown us how to read his body language. As is usual with Joel, we do not have the answers to his communication challenges, but we do have the tenacity to keep trying, to discover, to help, to suggest, and mostly—to love. Somehow, someway, he gets the point.

Typical Conversation:

Dad: Hey, Jordan, *Porgy and Bess* will be at Fair Park in Dallas at the end of February. Do you want to go?

Jordan: Sounds good to me.

Joel: What?

Dad: *Porgy and Bess* will be at Fair Park in Dallas. Are you interested in going also?

Joel: Maybe. Will there be an orchestra?

Dad: Yes

Joel: Will it be big?

Dad: I *think* so.

Joel: Will there be flutes?

Dad: Yes.

Joel: Clarinets?

Dad: Yes.

Joel: Oboes?

Dad: Yes.

Joel: Bassoons?

Dad: Yes.

Joel: Saxophones?

Dad: Not sure . . . but I think so.

Joel: Drums?

Dad: Yes.

Joel: Trumpets and Trombones?

Dad: Yes.

Joel: French Horns?

Dad: Yes.

Joel: Tubas?

Dad: Yes.

Joel: Violins and Violas and Cellos and the big, gigantic bass?

Dad: Yes, lots of instruments.

Joel: Will there be an organ?

Dad: I doubt it.

Joel: How come?

Dad: Usually, there is not an organ in an orchestra playing for a show, but I am not sure about this one.

Joel: What about a piano?

Dad: Maybe so.

Joel: Oh, good.

         (a moment of silence)

Joel: Will there be a tenor?

Dad: Yes, lots of singers.

Mom: Joel, it is an opera. Of course there will be tenors.

Joel: Lots of tenors?

Dad: Well . . . I think so.

Joel: How many tenors?

Dad: I don't know.

Joel: Probably, like about six or eight or ten tenors or twenty tenors.

Dad: Probably not that many.

Joel: A baritone?

Dad: Yes.

Joel: A soprano?

Dad: Yes. Probably a choir, too.

Joel: A big choir with lots of people?

Dad: Maybe, but not too big, since there is a stage.

Joel: How big is the choir?

Dad: Not sure, but it will be good.

Joel: How many are in the choir?

Dad: I really am not sure.

Joel: Who will be singing?

Dad: Not sure, but most of them will be of African-American descent like Gershwin intended.
(more silence)

Joel: How far away is it? Can we stay in a motel?

Dad: About three hours, but we will probably not stay in a motel.

Joel: I like motels with pools . . . indoor pools.

Dad: I know, but they cost money, and it will be enough just to pay for the show.

Joel: How much?

Dad: I am not sure yet.

Joel: About, like . . . $5.00?

Dad: More like $50 or $75 probably.

Joel: Oh! I have $50, but I want to buy a pin-stripe suit. Where will we eat?

Dad: Joel, I just don't know. It is not happening for several months, and we don't usually plan our eating places that far in advance.

Joel: Can we eat Mexican food?

Dad: Maybe so.

Joel: With lots of chips and tacos and enchiladas and hot sauce?

Dad: Probably, but let's not think about that right now.

Joel: Okay . . . What time will we leave?

Dad: Maybe three or so.

Joel: What should I wear?

Dad: Well, I guess nice clothes, but you don't need to worry about that right now.

Joel: Can I wear a tie?

Dad: Yes.

Joel: Should I wear a sweater, or maybe a black shirt and tie?

Dad: Yes, but since it is a long time, let's not talk about that. (long silence)

Joel: Are there lots of songs?

Dad: Yes, like "Bess, You Is My Woman Now" and "Summertime" and "I Got Plenty O' Nuttin".

Joel: Those are good songs.

Dad: Great songs.

Joel: Great songs. But I might not go.

Dad: (after thinking about that) Well, we'll talk more about it later.

Joel: But I might go.

Dad: Okay.

Joel: But I might stay home and eat Mexican food.

Dad: Maybe that is best.

Joel: But I want to see the orchestra.

Dad: Joel, let's talk more about this later. Right now it is time to eat.

Joel: Okay.

Thus was a typical conversation with our Joel when he was eighteen years old.

A low speaking voice could be the result of inactivity. Try to get your child/young adult into a physical activity to develop lung function, such as blowing up beach balls or balloons, and blowing on whistles could help, too.

Thirty-Two

Hygiene

Keeping clean and staying healthy are not natural instincts for an autistic child or adult. Autistics enjoy being clean and looking snappy in some ways, but the process for hygiene is mysterious and somehow deemed unnecessary. Once again, it requires careful teaching and consistent application to get the purpose and system of hygiene across to an autistic. Joel has always enjoyed taking a bath (as long as the water is not too hot) but not for the purpose of being clean, but, rather, for the feeling of being engulfed in water. As in other activities, we had to order the process of washing hair and body, rinsing thoroughly, and keeping with a time schedule. Without a timing system, the bath might take several hours. I recall the engaging movie titled, *Who's Afraid of Gilbert Grape,* about an autistic child and how an older brother looked out for his welfare. In the movie, there is one scene where the child stays in the bathtub for too many hours due to having been forgotten. He had the ability to get out of the tub but not the mental awareness of how long he had spent taking a bath.

For Joel, it is necessary to establish the routine and remind him of the importance of having good hygiene. This includes brushing his teeth, wearing deodorant, washing his hands, and using shampoo on his hair. At some point in his maturation, the value of being clean made a difference for him. Perhaps it was when his older brother pointed out the unkempt appearance or the body odor emanating from Joel. Maybe it was when someone mentioned his bad breath or turned away in concern at his lack of cleanliness, but for whatever reason, after many years of hard work, Joel, as an adult, generally practices good hygiene. We still have to remind him to wash up, brush his teeth, take a shower, and wash his hands, but aside from the occasional lapses, Joel has the best of intentions for staying clean and having good personal hygiene. We handle the laundry for him, but we do have to remind him not to wear the same clothes every day. Often, we make sure that he places his dirty clothes in the proper bin and that he is not "recycling" the same clothes out of a desire to look the same as the day before.

When we think about the social challenge of homeless citizens in our cities and throughout our country, we see adults in an unkempt condition walking around with poor hygiene and a lack of personal attention. Could it be that many of these people are autistic and simply do not have the awareness of their own condition, their odors, and the need for cleanliness? Is it as simple as not having a place to bathe or as much a problem of not recognizing their own effect upon others?

Would a social initiative for personal hygiene, a dispensing of toothbrushes and toothpaste, soap, clean clothes, a place for a shower, be appropriate for the care of the homeless or the indigent? Mostly we refer back to the need for education and awareness of the value of cleanliness for well-being. Because there are very few natural instincts for self-preservation in an autistic, it becomes central to find ways to teach and provide the basics of life. An essential trait for social and physical success is having the ability to be sanitary and clean. The alternative is to accept the burden of disease that will inevitably infect a person who does not know how to maintain personal hygiene.

Thirty-Three

Two Razors

He could not get past the fact that two razors instead of one were in the shower. It caused him great consternation, leading to a total interruption of the process of showering, resulting in emotional grief unlike anything experienced in a long time.

Joel relies on routine and established expectations for his general practice and behavior. Although somewhat flexible in certain situations, it is usually in circumstances where there is not an expected routine or expected ordering of events. Were we to set out on an adventure to the mall, to the lake, or to another city, since Joel is not sure of what to expect, he willingly accepts spontaneity. In those cases, he decides in advance that his world cannot be ordered, so it then becomes comfortable to adjust to the circumstances. Yet if he knows what to expect, has pre-ordered said events, and has prescribed the details in his mind, then his world gets turbulent when the system is altered.

He plans the event, unless the plan is not to have a plan. In a general sense, he enjoys knowing where we are going and what we are going to do, but he has no need to know the specifics. Yet we must be careful, because to present the specific information would be to set him up for despair. For example, we may take a trip to Abilene to go shopping. We leave this idea "open" to an extent so as not to have him order the shopping events and prescribe where we are going exactly, how we will proceed, and exactly what

135

will happen. To do so is to guarantee tension when the plans are altered. The plan then is to have no plan . . . which is fine with Joel.

But when there is a plan, and it is outlined specifically, then we must follow it. While routine is necessary in Joel's world, it can also be a little frustrating. Such was the case with the two razors in the shower.

Altering Joel's expectations creates a huge teeter-totter of insecurity and one that is only settled by putting the situation back in his control. Although he operates rationally and objectively, with decisions often devoid of emotion, when his expectations are not met, logical or rational explanations do not solve the problem. He sees the two razors in the shower, but expecting only one (and it must be the right one), he gets very upset and demands the removal of the wrong one. It is my suspicion that had we not removed the wrong one, he would have refused to shave and would have justified his refusal by the presence of the two razors.

Using the situation as a "teachable moment" would have been a total failure. While part of me wanted to explain that two razors are better than one, that two razors being there signifies the possibility that one is becoming dull, that he has the right to choose which one he wants, or that life doesn't always work out the way we want, I also recognized that simply removing the unwanted object would quickly solve the problem. So I did just that and all was well. He shaved and came out happy.

This razor event, however, was not all that surprising, considering the number of circumstances and unusual practices we have dealt with over the years. We never quite know what causes Joel's preferences for certain things, but we do respect his wishes as long as they are within the bounds of safety and appropriateness. He never wears shorts—only pants. He likes to eat chicken—as long as it does not have bones. He spent many years not eating hot dogs due to having choked on a hot dog when he was a child.

He will never eat another donut hole, because he found a hair on a donut hole when he was five years old. He only uses certain cups, hates tomatoes, loves salsa, hates fish, loves sausage, prefers solid colors, loves old movies, and dislikes Rock music. He only drinks RC Colas in plastic bottles, and at every athletic event we attend, he insists on eating an order of nachos with cheese. He also likes anything Italian, including food, people, music, and art. Each of these preferences and more can lead to an unpleasant event if we do not follow his desires. Since nothing is dangerous, we make an effort to meet his needs as much as possible, avoiding any kind of scene or emotional outburst. It is just easier that way. Unfortunately, sometimes things do happen, and it is our responsibility to help Joel when things are not right.

We continue to make an effort to educate Joel in how to deal with those happenstance events that are out of our and his control and to help him cope with the unexpected, to be flexible, and to "Make lemonade out of lemons." Yet, in spite of our continued and dedicated effort, there are times when the best approach is to fix the problem and go on. Such is the complicated world of parenting an autistic child. It can be quite entertaining, or quite frightening, but it is always something new.

Thirty-Four

More Texts

We continue to receive long texts from Joel that are both informative and useful:

'Hey dad is my coat that i bought at j.c. Penney back from the cleaners? I am wanting to wear it sunday at church! What are you going to wear this sunday dad? I am going to wear all black this sunday? It is supposed to get really cold this weekend! I think it is supposed to snow on sunday again! I am ready to have the ultimate snowball fight and build a really big snowman with sticks and a stick for a nose and a hat a scarf for buttons for eyes mouth and shirt and my tie around its neck! I am just ready to play the organ at church around jacob's spring break! I might play some easter hymns like christ the lord is risen today, crown him with many crowns, and it is well with my soul! I might want to do them for an easter medley! I am about to be on my way to HPU here in a few minutes! I will see you in fifteen minutes! I am just about to get a drink of water and head out of here! I will ttyl bye father!!!!!!! :-)'

I notice that he is foregoing the capitalization process in his texts, although he still needs to be complete in everything else. The ttyl is a good sign overall, I think. While I miss the precision a little (since that was part of the charm of Joel's earlier texts), I think his lack of precision is actually a good sign. It has been said by Temple Grandin that autism improves slowly over a period of time. I believe this is due to the ability to cope and find ways to fit into a world that otherwise does not make sense . . . sort of an ability to be a successful actor in order for others to accept you into their world.

Perhaps Joel is discovering a way to pretend that he is normal and is finding a way to adjust to the strange world in which he finds himself. Texting keeps him in touch with his family and friends, connecting to them on a verbal plane without having to vocalize.

Thirty-Five

Memory, Traveling, and Order

While traveling to see our oldest son, we pulled into the parking lot in Weatherford, Texas between Wendy's and Starbucks. It must have struck a memory tone for Joel, because he proceeded to tell me with great excitement about all the shops in the area. He said that two years earlier we had parked in the same place. I never know what will trigger his brain into activity. Certain sparks of memory, sound, places, or events seem to hyperdrive or give him a brain turbo boost.

Trying to figure Joel out is always an adventure. Will it ever happen? Doubtful . . . but the journey to that end is filled with joy!

Joel's world is ordered. Without a sense of order, Joel has trouble functioning. As pointed out earlier, he can accept a certain amount of ambiguity, provided it is planned ambiguity. For example, the bus picks him up every day between 12:15 and 1:30. It would be ideal to establish the precise time of pickup, but, unfortunately, the system does not allow for that. Yet Joel is comfortable knowing that it will happen within that established framework, planning for the somewhat nebulous time for arrival.

But, overall, he needs order to find meaning and cannot live in a constant state of confusion or randomness. This weakness, if indeed it is a weakness, is related to his lack of creativity and imagination. Looking at this from another direction, with some exceptions, people with a messy desk, car, or who lead a spontaneous lifestyle generally have a greater degree of personal creativity and imagination. Obviously, this generalization has a consequence in that extremes are rarely beneficial in any sense.

As an aside, I knew a very creative but dysfunctional musician whose lifestyle and personal habits were completely without order, resulting in total physical and personal messes without any kind of productivity at any time. It ultimately caused his health and career demise, demonstrating how any extreme rarely has any gain.

Joel, however, being uncomfortable with spontaneity, missing an imagination, and not developing a sense of dreams, replaces this ingredient with a need for order amidst the chaos of the world. Loving to travel but needing to know where, how long, what to bring, and what the trip entails, he packs accordingly and specifically. Obviously this is not an unusual trait, for many people prefer to pack fastidiously, planning for their trip and any contingencies.

Where Joel differs is in his system of packing and determining the items for the trip. He lays out his clothes in order of days, sets out his personal items, creates a spot for other things—Italian dictionary for example, counts the items within the stacks, and packs accordingly. He then applies the number needed, exacting the items numerically. This means that if he has packed eight personal items on the trip, then there is something missing, since there should be nine. He then seeks out the ninth item . . . whatever that may be. While most people simply make sure their deodorant is present, he, instead, numbers it among the nine personal items needed. After counting the total, he then seeks out the precise number of the item.

When we were returning to Texas from North Carolina on a recent trip, he was somewhat perplexed since item number seven was missing. Thinking it through, he found item number seven, a razor, in the shower. This completed the total and allowed him to finish packing for the return trip. His system works for him and demonstrates his continued need for order and systems. He is lacking in creativity and imagination, and yet it is easy to see that he simply rewrites the definitions of those terms according to his own needs. It seems to me that it takes imagination to organize his life by his system. We may not always understand it, but we do respect it.

Reasoning with Joel based on common sense procedures is a difficult endeavor due to his inability to accept cause and effect. He cannot understand how to improve efficiency, comfort, or ease of practice. When one method has worked, whether our perception of success would be different or not, Joel tends to stay with that method regardless of the circumstances. As responsible guardians, we continue to walk the tightrope of giving him latitude and allowing him to make his own mistakes, hoping he will learn from the situation and improve the next time. We often remind him of ways to improve, of things to consider, of various methods to make his life easier, quicker, and more convenient, but, unfortunately, his natural inclination is to keep it the same way regardless of its efficacy.

We do have ways, however, of helping Joel deal with his general lack of common sense and awareness. We translate the experience into some kind of order, often using numbers to demonstrate the need. Rather than saying, "Go pack your bag for the upcoming trip," we will instead say, "Go count the number of items you require for the upcoming trip." We then later remind him to pack the exact number needed. Obviously, there are potential problems with this system, in that he may leave something out or not count a needed item and yet insist that he has the correct number. But the upside of this system is that he is able to order things in his mind and simplify the overriding goal into one aggregate.

Being autistic is often overwhelming, with the sheer plethora of information coming at you constantly. An autistic cannot process everything around him quickly or easily, and it becomes a tornado of sounds, sights, and images that have little or no cohesiveness in their delivery. The opportunity to reduce the unnecessary, paring down the essential information into a number or numbers, is blissful to an autistic. This is true for nearly all situations, circumstances, and goals. We help him order his goals, aiming for one final number to be considered as the main goal or purpose. When we express the objectives, the plans, and the expectations in terms of a number, Joel's eyes light up, and he quickly comprehends what is about to happen. He may not always understand how the ordered numbers work together to accomplish the necessary goal, but he is willing to and excited about taking those exact steps.

Sometimes this requires a great deal of specificity, but at other times, it can be expressed in generalities. The more specific the expression, the better quality will be the results. Conversely, the more general the list, the more breadth of accomplishment is performed. If cleaning his room is the requirement, we will see more accomplishment by listing the order of how to make that happen, "Joel, do five things: 1) Make your bed, 2) Pick up your clothes and put them in the hamper, 3) Place your shoes in your closet, 4) Stack your games on the night stand, 5) Pick up any papers or trash on the floor and place them in the trash can." We then follow up with, "Joel, please do those five things: bed, clothes, shoes, games, trash." We then anticipate success.

Or, we could try the old unsuccessful method: (LOUD VOICE) "Joel, go clean up your room now, and do it right!" In a frustration moment, we might start listing all the things that should happen to get the room cleaned, but without a strict order of events, to an autistic it will feel like standing in an anthill wondering what is happening or a storm of oobleck falling upon his head and

144

making everything sticky. The clarity of numbers provides clarity of thought for Joel.

We have learned to get his attention by taking away distractions, presenting the overall goal and purpose, and then ordering and numbering the events. We wish we could always apply a timetable to the instructions, but time remains a mysterious abstraction to Joel and likely always will. With this in mind, we allow greater time for accomplishment than would normally be needed and continually ask ourselves for patience, wisdom, and clarity.

Thirty-Six

Autistics and Sexuality

S exual desire cannot be denied, even for autistic teenagers, but because of the socialization process, a process that is mysterious for autistics, sexual desire is natural rather than forced. This makes for an awkward enculturation and a confusion of responses. How should he react?

Although heavily debated, there is no doubt that beauty is a shared response of collective wisdom and current trends. We notice that oil paintings in the 16th century and earlier portray women to be rather curvy, often with layers of fat that we would now consider excessive. Since an autistic teenager does not learn from the socialization around him, his reactions to beauty are devoid of external influences . . . at least to an extent. He learns by what he feels or is able to assimilate objectively. The curious need for truth and precision collides with the artistic need for beauty. This means that his sexual responses are not governed by what others tell him or what the media portrays but instead are led from within.

Joel does not seek thin, bikini-clad blondes with large bosoms; instead, he responds, but not necessarily sexually, to young ladies who are nice to him. They are not always beautiful by modern standards but instead have the kind of authentic pleasantry that he seeks in people. This makes him separate the physical from the personal. Perhaps all of us intend this in our social circles, yet

147

I suspect if the truth were revealed, we would discover a latent sexual agenda in many people.

For Joel, and likely for many autistics, he is a sexual being not dependent on the looks of the opposite sex. It really means nothing to him, and he is not able to judge anyone on the basis of appearance. His sexual desires are normal and are a result of growing up, not a result of what anyone has told him, and not a result of the media. He is, in fact, disturbed by nudity and not comfortable around the flirty kind of physical response of teenagers. Flirting is a behavior that must be inferred by the recipient, but Joel does not understand inference, making flirting a confusing act. He cannot comprehend the hidden meaning in the act, cannot act that way himself, and, therefore, does not understand such behavior.

It is refreshing to know that his sexuality is not dependent on seeing inappropriate pictures or watching a beautiful young lady, but that it is a natural growth of what is in him. While he cannot determine what the future holds, we are certain that he is not driven by the media's description of sex appeal. This is comforting for us. Now we need to help him understand himself—a far taller order.

Avoid sexual humor or subtle sexual references.
An autistic will likely not understand these and will
simply be confused, not knowing how to respond in any sense.

Thirty-Seven

Adjusting and Coping

U sing every educational technique available to us, as do all caring parents, we try to convince Joel what to do and how to adjust. This was true when he was just a child and remains true today. Often it seems hopeless, while at other times it actually happens, but we hold our breaths when he won't be convinced.

Some of the problem is his stubbornness, a character trait that is not unique to autistics and certainly not applied to all children with autism. He gets locked into an idea and will not let go of the concept regardless of the level of reasoning presented. Once it is in his head, that is the way it is, and no amount of convincing otherwise will alter that idea. It makes for extremely stressful moments and arguments without a good result.

Is it his personality? Is it due to autism? Is it the lack of maturation or cognitive development? Perhaps a combination of all these leads to the behavior. Joel has times of compliance and acceptance of the circumstances around him, but he has other times of resistance. It is the resistant times that make our lives difficult and remind us of the ongoing challenges of raising an autistic child.

Do you need some examples? Okay, here you go: Shower time—always a battle. He has no conception of time and often lets the shower run for twenty to thirty minutes without getting in. This means that we have to monitor him to get it done.

Clothes—he insists on dressing up, including a tie, even on days when it is not appropriate, such as to a football game. Playing the organ—he believes it is his right and obligation to practice every day after work. Some days don't allow for that, so he gets very upset about the change in schedule. It is the little things, like wanting an RC Cola in a bottle, not a can, and refusing to open it for one or two days, or packing for a trip a week early, or eating a whole bag of chips and hot sauce, or pouring half the chocolate syrup into the milk. All these and more tend to become major battles of concern for him. While we often give in for the sake of harmony, at other times, we work to teach him why it is best to do something different.

Yet the truth remains: If he is not receptive to reason, then all reasoning is in vain, so we try to get him to calm down, think rationally, see the bigger picture, and be less contentious about his own preconceived ideas. We try and sometimes succeed. This has been true for twenty years.

So, it is a puzzle as to why Joel still has moments where he is insistent on certain things, regardless of our efforts to convince him otherwise. It makes for tension and stress that most families rarely experience. I suspect he will have these moments for the rest of his life. Luckily, however, they do seem to be diminishing in frequency and in length. They are just something for us to handle and to always be aware of the potential of such times.

Tip:

At larger high schools, talk to the counselor about having a "circle of friends" for the autistic student. This group will look out for him, watch for bullying or others trying to take advantage of him, and act as models for appropriate behavior and as problem solvers.

Thirty-Eight

The Middle Name Conundrum

We have never quite been able to discern the reason for his abhorrence, but the fact has remained for years that he just does not like his middle name. It is Arlitt—Joel Arlitt Tucker. Arlitt is a family name of German descent whose members eventually settled in large numbers throughout much of Texas. It is a name to lift up and be proud, a name signifying strength and success. But he does not like it, never has, and we do not know why.

Finally, in a fit of mild rage, Joel asked why everyone else has a middle name that begins with a consonant while his begins with a vowel. Often, Joel's unusual statements that come out of the blue leave us perplexed, curious as to what he means, and desperately wishing we could get inside his head to learn more. His statement about consonants and vowels was different, causing us to stare at him in wonderment. Further questioning revealed that everyone he knows has a middle name that begins in a consonant and that it is not fair that his middle name begins with a vowel. He then said he prefers consonants over vowels.

I don't believe he hates vowels and probably looks at vowels as fillers for the rest of the word, but, obviously, he is more comfortable with consonants. I have known ranchers who preferred goats over sheep but didn't necessarily hate the sheep but did certainly like goats better. I guess that is another story though. Anyway, for whatever reason, Joel prefers consonants over vowels and wishes his middle name started with a consonant. I threw out some options, none of which made any sense. Particularly, starting Arlitt with an H was disconcerting!

Finally, I explained to Joel that had we known of his preference, we would not have named him Arlitt. He did not seem to understand this at all. Perhaps it is his lack of time understanding, or the strange idea that what he thinks, he assumes everyone thinks, or maybe that nobody in his right mind would want a middle name that starts with a vowel. Whatever the reason, he correctly blames us for the poor naming job we did years ago.

I suspect this problem will remain forever, and other than not using his name or even referencing or making a legal request, I do not think this situation will change. In some ways, however, it is simply another example of how Joel must learn to cope with things that do not meet his expectations. In truth, life is often like that, whether one is autistic or not. Unfortunately, it becomes exaggerated for autistics.

I once heard of an autistic adult who hated Texas (That is hard for me to believe!) and refused to look at it on a map. His hatred was real to him, and because of his emotion, the family could never visit the state. Families of autistics make adjustments, alter their lives, and make sacrifices which normal families would never make. It is all a part of finding the child where he lives and working diligently to help him cope in a strange world. For the family who could never visit the State of Texas, there are plenty of other great states to visit.

Thirty-Nine

Understanding Autism

S itting in McDonald's this morning and enjoying a cup of coffee, I am reminded of the time many years ago when I came to this same establishment with a friend and two of my boys, Joel and Jordan. They were quite young, maybe three and six or so, with Joel being the oldest. My friend and I decided to get a cup of coffee, and I thought the boys would enjoy a pancake and orange juice.

After taking their orders, getting their drinks, and setting them down in a booth, I returned to the counter to get the rest of the food. Suddenly, I and everyone in McDonald's heard a bloodcurdling scream that made everyone jump, while fearing the worst. It seems that Joel and Jordan were having an altercation in the manner that most boys have, particularly brothers (Believe it or not, I had a few with my brother here and there.). It was sort of a variation on property rights and seat location: "I want to sit here!" "No, this is my spot!" "My juice is here!" "That's my juice," etc. While we try to teach our children about the improper time and place for altercations, and we certainly want to instill in our children a sense of public decorum, they do not always subscribe to the adult models.

We have all experienced the bad behavior of children, and we inevitably find ourselves in judgment over the handling of that behavior. Rather than blame the child, we generally look at the parent in disgust, wondering why that parent cannot handle the situation better. There may be a part of us that knows children are unpredictable and that even the finest parenting skills cannot solve all problems, yet we still tend to pass judgment, in a form of removal and assigning responsibility. This is a major issue facing parents of autistic children and one that will be addressed later.

Back to the problem at hand . . . Joel's inappropriate scream was beyond that of a normal six year old frustrated with his brother. It was a scream disproportionate to the situation, a variation of the schizophrenic emotional outburst not matching the stimulus. Whatever—it was loud and scary. In a mixture of horror and amusement, I quickly moved to the boys, hugged Joel to get him calmed down, solved the problem, and assuaged the grave concerns of the customers present. All was well.

This scene is typical of the kind of thing we have always faced as parents of an autistic child. Joel could not contain, and still has trouble containing, his emotional reactions. When a situation did not match his expectations, when the order became disordered, when the prescription failed, he reacted in the extreme. We did not know when that would happen or even what to do. But it taught us to be prepared, to work at meeting his expectations, and to remain isolated when possible. Medication has helped him, but he still struggles a bit with this, now manifesting itself in other challenges.

We learned patience, preparation, and protection in our raising of Joel. This is part of the joy and sorrow of having an autistic child.

Too often, we spend our time reacting to other people, particularly those we love, being angry at their flaws, or hopefully loving their positive qualities. For those outside our immediate circle, we may be envious, or admiring, or full of disdain, but we rarely seem to understand or sympathize with their situation or even their own emotional condition. No, I am not teaching tolerance here; I am, instead, advocating a deeper understanding of human nature . . . of autistics in particular.

When dealing with autistics, whether they are very small children or adults, rather than criticizing, perhaps we should be empathizing, or, to take it another step further, maybe it is time for many of us to look at the world through the eyes of the challenged. The recent passing of a friend who was a blind trumpet player prompted me again to imagine a world without sight. How must that be? Each day, I depend on my sight and my mind to process that which I see, from people, to things, to this computer, and to the vast array of colors, shapes, and symbols that cross my path almost minute by minute. Not to have sight presents a world of darkness and imagination that must be entirely different from what sighted people experience daily.

I am not convinced that we, as the loving parents of our autistic son, have ever truly understood his perspective on life. Sometimes I am not sure who he really is, in fact. How does his brain process information? What does he see, hear, or feel? We have worked so hard to help him cope and fit into this crazy world that maybe we have missed a thorough comprehension of Joel's inner sanctum. Yet while it is easy to acknowledge this possibility, it is far more challenging to fix the problem of "Who is Joel?"

I recall choosing one of those odd shopping carts a few weeks ago that seemed to have a steering problem. While dwelling on the pitiful emotion of, *Why do I always get the bad buggy?* I began to compensate for its flaws. Yes, I would have preferred a little more ease of mobility, and, yes, I had to use a touch of elbow grease to make it work well, but, on the other hand, it was better than having to carry cereal, coffee, meat, bread, and canned goods in my arms. The little cart struggled some, but we worked together and came to some positive resolutions! Perhaps it was later repaired, or perhaps someone else came along and shared in the challenging joy of steering the little guy.

At first, I was frustrated that my cart did not work the way I had hoped. My concept of shopping carts did not include a bad wheel.

But I compensated for the situation, and, after a while, I almost did not notice the problem. Unlike Joel, however, the cart could be repaired, or at least be given a new wheel. Joel cannot get a new brain. He may, one day, have the opportunity to have it repaired (I think we are many years away from that kind of biotechnology.), but, for now, he simply has to adjust for the inherent situation in which he lives. As his parents and guardians, we work to steer him in such a way as to stay on course and accomplish his goals, but, ultimately, he has to find a way to direct himself.

Since this is true, it is frustrating, and, in many ways, it is futile to resist and try to change those characteristics that make Joel who he is. What does work is our seeking to embrace his qualities and approach him in the way he approaches life, avoiding the abstract, creating an environment of trust, keeping things ordered and pleasant, and recognizing his limitations. This makes for a healthier and happier theater for him. A principle of teaching is somewhere in this essay—find him where he is and help him accomplish those things that will benefit him the most.

As Joel entered the working world at the age of nineteen, having graduated from high school, it occurred to me that we had spent a great deal of time and energy in educating him concerning how to act, respond, behave, learn, and "fit in" to the world as a contributing adult and member of society. To an extent, at least within the confines of his disability, he is able to do just that.

Yet all is not 'peachy' in the Joel world, for many people do not know what to do or how to help him adjust. To that end, I write this essay for business owners, employers, managers, various employees, and all those in the workplace who are willing to take a chance on a disabled adult and help guide him toward success in a career or simply to know how to respond to Joel, and people like Joel, when you encounter them in everyday life.

One major thing to remember is to have patience and to allow time for normal events. This includes ordering food, writing checks, walking, crossing the street, sorting, carrying packages, getting on buses, and responding to questions. A good rule of thumb is to double the normal time for all activities and avoid rushing the process, which would lead to undue stress and a possible lack of productivity. A second problem for autistic adults is in the area of communication. While they often know the answer and may even perceive the situation accurately, they likely will be unable to express their own needs. This can be very frustrating for the disabled adult as well as for the employer or helper, and a guessing game often results as you try to discern the need or the problem. When this happens, try using pictures or even a form of charades to determine the desired behavior.

Autistic adults thrive better in quiet, ordered environments. While they are very social (forget the old myth of autistics preferring solitude), they also tend to become agitated and confused in overly-loud, complex environments. Within this quiet, ordered environment is the need for routine, clear expectations, only one thing at a time, and without unnecessary interruptions. Autism lends itself to excelling in one or two disciplines, thereby resulting in a type of "expert" behavior. Finding this specialization may be challenging, but once it becomes apparent, the autistic adult can actually be considered superior in that particular area.

In Joel's case, he excels at putting things in order and finds libraries perfectly suited to his personality and his ordered universe. The quiet but hidden creative world of books that are begging to be found and can only be found if cataloged and placed in the correct spots have a diligent and dedicated friend in Joel Tucker who remains committed to ordered perfection for their domicile. The books smile when Joel enters the library, for they know he will ensure their safe passage to their rightful place. Although his pace is somewhat adagio, and his music tends to be soft, his melody is pleasant and the rhythm ordered with excellent goals. His productivity may not be as high as that of other people, but it is accurate, tasteful, fastidious, and objective. In the right kind of setting, Joel can and will be successful.

Mostly, it is essential to watch out for those who cannot seem to grasp what is normally mundane. A trip to the grocery store, to the convenience store, to the mall, or virtually anywhere, will be eye-opening when you begin to look for anyone struggling. It could be a physical limitation, a mental limitation, or simply something that just does not make sense. Sometimes autistics appear to be normal until you see them dealing with something that is normally easy for most people. For example, since autistics prefer to keep things in some kind of order, it is frustrating to them to remove something from the shelf without keeping the other items in order. Many times we will see Joel staring at an item, wondering how to remove it without changing the system.

Also, remember that an autistic struggles with sound filtering, so if an announcement occurs over a loudspeaker or someone says something important, to an autistic, it is simply another sound. They tend to hear everything the same and cannot discern one sound from another. They may not hear or understand, "Closing in fifteen minutes," or, "Please evacuate the building," or, "All bananas are now on sale!" These kinds of general announcements to everyone else often do not have meaning to an autistic.

As we go through our lives, we need to learn to look out for those who struggle, for those who may not understand the obvious, and for those who need special kinds of help. Patience and clear communication is needed for autistics as they work to cope in a difficult world.

Just read about the mother who strangled her two autistic children, claiming that she couldn't handle them anymore. In her demented mind, she seemed to think that their behavior justified her own horrific actions. Plus, she insisted that we try to understand her plight, her fears, her situation, that we place ourselves in her position. But try as we might, killing our own children, regardless of their disability, is beyond comprehension.

Assuming her madness, the extreme state of her fragile mind, her feelings of hopelessness, and her desire to escape her cage of parental responsibility, we still wonder at a woman who had nowhere to turn, who gave up, who sought no help, who destroyed the very lives she had brought into the world.

But rather than focus on the mother, let's take a moment to think about the children. Not knowing enough particulars to speak accurately, I feel a need to remind people that nobody wants to be autistic. This is neither a desirable trait nor a choice. Children are not born hoping to be autistic. It is not a profession, an ambition, or a dream in any sense. Autism is a disability that continues to afflict millions of children and adults. Unlike poor judgment or indecision, autism is not something that a child takes upon himself for attention, desire, or success. It is not something to be rewarded or affirmed in the sense of, "You are doing such a great job of being autistic." It is not a desirable disability. Children don't want it, and parents do not want it for their children.

But it happens. It doesn't always happen to other people; it can happen to your children or your grandchildren. It is not an abstract, albeit oddly fascinating event that we read about in Science Fiction books or watch in movies hoping to learn a little about the curious disability known as autism. It is real, and those afflicted are around you.

A child with autism cannot suddenly change himself, rid himself of the disability, or pretend to understand the outside world. The world is a mystery compounded by the inability to adjust easily to the social norms of culture. Social contractarianism, a process children learn as they grow, is without any kind of meaning to a child with autism. It is a tough existence for a child as well as for a parent, working hard to find a way to cope in a world that is entirely different from the world inside the head.

161

But there is also good news: There is a lot of help for parents and for children suffering with autism. While it is vastly difficult, and at times seemingly hopeless, in reality, hope is prevalent and only a phone call, email, book, or video away. For those whose lives are filled with despair with seemingly nowhere to turn, I encourage you to find a support group and learn how to help your child adjust. To the mother who destroyed her children as well as her own soul, perhaps the only good is the reminder that autism is serious and that we should always urge those suffering to avoid the same vicious trappings of loneliness and hopelessness. Seek help. There are many who want to help.

When faced with a situation, stay calm but work quickly to get the child away from other people and away from the situation.

Forty

Routine

Joel requires routine in his life. He needs the routines that establish the order of events and give him a sense of stability and love. Without a system, a sequential approach to daily living, he becomes uncomfortable, insecure, edgy, fearful, and emotionally distraught. While this is generally true for all people, it is even more pronounced for an autistic child.

Routines do not have to be, nor should they be, restrictive. They, instead, should give unification to a world that appears to be a random mess. Very little about the world makes sense to an autistic person. It all seems nebulous, frightening, unusual, and completely unpredictable. Very little stays the same every day, and it all appears to have changed from the day before. This makes for an existence that could be paranoid and schizophrenic. Instead, many autistics simply prefer a withdrawn personality that is absolutely trusting when confronted. This appears to be ironic at first look, but it makes sense in the thought processing of an autistic. If the world is scary, why not deny it and live happily in your own existence, rejecting those things that are threatening? An odd attitude, but think of it this way: if you see a black widow spider, you know to stay away from it. If you see a black widow spider, turn away, and then turn back, you hope to see it again. But if you don't, then you ought to be nervous.

But the autistic is not only *not* nervous, he is also no longer aware of the existence of the spider in the world. "Out of sight, out of mind," is the practice for an autistic. Because of this lack of a concept of danger, the next time he sees the spider or any spider, it poses no threat in his mind. I suppose that if the spider bit him, he would then be hesitant about spiders, but that is a learned response from experience, not from instincts. Not that he is unaware of danger entirely (although you should know that there is very little instinctual awareness of danger in an autistic's makeup), for he knows to look both ways when crossing a street, and the bark of dog is a little frightening to him, in general, he trusts everyone and all things. It makes for a happy, unaware existence, and one in which all of us are envious in many ways.

I recall the children's story about the sister who told her parents that her brother had "talked to a stranger." The father was horrified and proceeded to tell his little boy about the dangers of strangers and the awful things that could happen to him. The boy became frightened of everyone and everything, and the world then looked like a dark, foreboding place at every turn. The mother, of course, fixed this by pointing out the good things in the world and how it is wise to be cautious and a little wary at times, but, for the most part, life is grand and we should not be frightened of everyone. A funny little story to remind us to look at the world optimistically when we can but not to avoid realism when necessary.

For Joel, and many autistics, he cannot see the world realistically but, instead, sees it under a different lens, a view that is ordered, positive, comfortable, rosy, and predictable. But getting back to the routine idea, Joel needs an ordered system to provide a strong sense of stability to his world. Without it, all is frightening, dark, cloudy, mysterious, and confusing.

We have established the need for routine in dealing with autistic children, and this idea really does not change from childhood into adulthood. Often the routines alter, but the important thing to remember is to keep to the routine even in the variation. For years, composers have used a technique in music called "variation technique" which allows for the music to alter in different ways, often substantially, or, in some cases, minimally, yet maintains some kind of unifying element to the original theme. The melody may stay the same; the harmony may stay the same, the rhythm, or something that recalls the original theme. This same idea can be practiced in dealing with autism.

We practice routines in order to give Joel stability in the world, something familiar that takes away the deep fears that may be within him. The routine makes the statement that all is well, that all will be fine, and that the world is the same place that it was yesterday. The event may alter slightly, and it may be varied from how it was yesterday, but it retains enough similarities to give it the familiarity needed.

For several years now, Joel and I have some routines, and while they do change some, they have more or less remained. "Hey, Joel," I say. "Hey, Dad," he responds. We do this every day and have for years. After his shower, he comes out with wet hair, and I always say, "Joel, it is time to take a—" Joel always completes the sentence with a fast, "Shower." This routine started with me pretending to be shocked that he had actually taken a shower. It now is a necessary game that happens every night.

Other routines include the thumbs up to each other, the comical face to him, the broken finger game, the "I swallowed a pencil" joke, and the list goes on and on. All these things and more provide an absolutely necessary sense of order for Joel. Other things, such as brushing teeth, combing hair, putting on clothes, tying shoes, washing hands, are all part of the routine of the day. We also enjoy the odd wave that occurs at a distance. This is a funny one, since Joel will wave at me regardless of where I am or what I am doing.

Joel also develops routines with friends, including, "How tall are you?" or special handshakes, or text messaging. All these and more serve as reminders to him that the world is stable, that love surrounds him, that there may be some bad things, but that the good things happen every day. Joel's need to hear music, to play music, and talking to his family adds to the ever-present need for routine and familiarity.

For the non-autistic, such routines could become commonplace, dull, lacking in spirit, or missing the element of spontaneity. Most of us seek adventure in some form or another. But for the autistic, adventure is not found in the new; it is found in the comfortable.

The use of "Social Stories", stories written by the parent or teacher that use the child as the main character to describe appropriate and expected behavior, is very effective for higher-functioning autistics.

Forty-One

Facial Expressions and Reading Emotions

Have you ever wondered why married couples begin to look like each other over a period of years? Have you ever watched couples in their seventies and eighties who have been married over fifty years who could pass for brother and sister? It is sort of eerie and a little frightening at times. Why does this happen?

It has to do with facial expressions. After years of staring at each other and learning each other's facial changes, we begin to take on the facial expressions of the partner. This then results in a similar look and response to the same stimuli. While at first married couples retain individuality, eventually, the give and take of relationships shows up in a sharing of facial expressions. Fascinating, to say the least.

Take a few minutes to think of your own facial expressions in response to certain stimuli. Do you react the same when alone as you do in public? If you are being seen by someone or are in a group, do you demonstrate the same face as you do in private? Doubtful. We are all products of the social environment in which we reside. We may not intend to demonstrate a particular face or respond in a certain way to external stimuli, but everyone does. Do we react exactly the same way when alone? Joel does. He does not put on a face to prove his emotions to others. His facial expressions are natural and not contrived in any sense. He is not trying to impress anyone at anytime. He simply acts and looks according to his own inside theater, devoid of external pressures of social norms. While sociologists and psychologists disagree about the nature of facial expressions, as to whether they are learned, cultural, or innate, the truth is that we respond to others and express ourselves through our facial expressions.

Unknown to him, I watched him one night in his room as he was in bed getting ready to go to sleep. He was talking to himself and obviously concerned about a couple of things. I think I heard something about getting Mexican food and not steak at a restaurant (He always prefers Mexican food over everything else.). As he expressed himself, his face did alter some, nothing dramatic but certainly obvious to me. And yet his face did not match his words, at least in the normal social expectations. He registers emotions, but it is not easy to tell what the emotions are.

Most of us have developed expressions matching our situation, or at least demonstrating what we want others to know. In some instances, I might hide my emotions with a false smile, or I might even pretend to be upset for a reason (like when my children would sneak cookies before dinner), or I might feign confusion in order for the person to clarify the statement. Yet all these facial expressions are somewhat manipulative, or at least artificial, to an extent. Other times, our faces simply register honest feelings—fear, joy, love, stress, pain, etc.

Yet an autistic person does not benefit from knowing what those faces should be. He does not develop particular expressions to match his emotions. Therefore, what you see is what is likely the most natural, devoid of any kind of social contract theory. It makes for great difficulty in assessing the feelings of the individual.

Joel recently acquired a new cell phone. It is sleek, fancy, full of games, has a nice screen, and is generally very advanced. He said he liked it, and I believed him, but his face did not display that pleasure. We are used to this, having experienced years of opening presents without hearing or seeing the joy that normally comes from that. Yet it was a little disconcerting to me. So I asked him forthrightly if he liked his phone. He said yes, and I told him I wish he would express his joy and happiness. He thought for a minute and then jumped three times with his hands in the air. That was good enough for me and made me laugh.

We should not be deceived by the lack of "accurate" and expected facial expressions to emotions. Autistics do not and will not respond according to a social norm. But they do experience emotions, strong ones, and they do have joys, sorrow, fear, and a plethora of feelings like any other human. Yet their feelings are not manifest in facial expressions typical of our expectations.

Now let's discuss body language. We are told that body language is as much as 80% of communication. Others say the number is closer to 50%. We are talking about the use of body language in communication. Whatever the truth, for an autistic, the number is considerably lower. For one thing, an autistic person generally has trouble physically. Their gait is sometimes awkward; their muscles are slow to develop; their eye-hand coordination is weak, and their physiological makeup is rather behind. It makes for physical challenges, that while not debilitating, are certainly limiting. And yet, with that aside, an autistic learner does not have the ability to perceive or deliver appropriate body language, except on an obviously basic level.

If half of our communication and our ability to understand others is physical body language, then it stands to reason that an autistic is already at a huge disadvantage in communicating and/ or understanding others. Add to this a disadvantage with regard to verbal skills, creativity, and imagination, and it is easy to see how tough it becomes to communicate on any kind of expected level.

If crossing your arms signifies disagreement or wanting to place a barrier between you and the other person, Joel never disagrees or wants barriers. If eye contact signifies confidence, or in some cases defiance, then Joel has neither, since he has serious trouble making eye contact. His body does not manifest his emotional state. An autistic does not see or read other people's body language and does not act out his own. He physically responds in a pragmatic way to the events of the moment.

Because body language is another kind of expression of imagination or creativity, it makes sense that Joel cannot experience the complexities of such. He is pretty much missing the gene that gives him creativity. Remember that he cannot lie since lying requires imagination, and he cannot fabricate a body language that matches his mood, whether on purpose or by instinct. This is not to say that he won't do the occasional "Hummph" with his eyes closed and arms crossed. We have seen that but find it to be suspiciously like a cartoon.

Body language, unless deliberate, tends to be, at least for most people, subtle and nondescript, a small extension of the circumstances of the moment. When we fear something or are embarrassed, we tend to hide our faces in our hands. When our favorite team scores a touchdown, we throw our arms open in an expression of glee. When we hear something important, we lean forward, or in boredom we begin to look around. These are commonplace reactions that seem innate, although perhaps they are learned behaviors as well. None of these actions happen with autistics.

For Joel, he does not have enough complexity of expression to add to his physiology. It is enough for him to understand the event, the request, or the emotion, without having to supplement it with enhanced body language. If he does not like the food, he simply will not eat it. If he sees someone he knows, he simply approaches that person with a handshake, hug, or wave. His body language is natural and obvious, containing no deceit, no manipulation, and no subtleties—just plain, honest, simple expression without complexity. This does not mean that Joel is devoid of emotion, approaching life entirely objectively, preferring a stoic existence, or a rigid approach in a kind of black and white existence dealing with facts only. No, Joel is very colorful and emotional, but he does not display this in the same way we do. Instead, he is very cognizant of his differences as per his disability. Therefore, he generally appears to be rather cold and lacking in expression.

Please be aware that as autistic children mature, they tend to become less emotive and more protective. This is a form of maturity. Much of it is the often sad awareness that we don't always get everything we want in life. In a way, that is part of the maturation process for everyone.

The lack of perception of reality in an autistic requires parents and teachers to present reality using visuals that are easily understood and well-organized. Always avoid abstract statements and instead support your lesson with concrete visual examples.

Forty-Two

Awareness of His Disability

We have never tried to hide Joel's disabilities from him, but, instead, we have sought to help him through them while constantly encouraging improvement. To remind him continually that he cannot do certain things due to being disabled would become self-fulfilling, causing him to wake up every day knowing he is different and unable to make any kind of effort at anything. On the other side, however, it never has seemed right to affirm him and postulate dreams that cannot happen. Filling his head with goals that are unattainable is a form of abuse and is not fair.

So we avoid either kind of extreme and instead deal with Joel realistically, pragmatically, yet with non-stop encouragement of the things he can do. For example, Joel cannot drive, and we do not expect him to ever be able to do so. He tends to focus on one thing, being totally unaware of other things around him. He also cannot filter or organize sounds, making road noise a constant roar in his mind. Further, manipulating a steering wheel, blinkers, brakes, and accelerator would be too many instruments to do at one time, not to mention the fact that anything moving quickly overwhelms him.

Recognizing this as truth, he never asks to drive, and we never say things like, "When you learn to drive, you can . . ." It would fill him with false dreams on the level of someone telling me I will become a professional basketball player someday. Some things just won't happen.

Yet, our knowing and reminding him of his limitations is not degrading or negative. Instead, we continually replace the problems with his potential. About once a week, we ask him to list the things he does successfully—playing the organ, sorting books, helping in the kitchen, choosing clothes, sharing good cheer and friendliness, and learning about actors and musicals. All these and more form a complete person and provide a sense of self-worth. While occasionally we have to gently say no to something he wants to do, we always try to find an opportunity to say yes to something else.

He mentions his disability occasionally but avoids the use of the term autistic. We are not sure why, but it reminds us not to tell people he is autistic in front of him. He doesn't mind our telling people he is disabled, as long as we do so judiciously and without criticism. We do not advertise this fact openly but are not embarrassed about it either. We and Joel work hard to appear "normal", but often his disability becomes obvious when carrying out tasks in public. Because of this, it often helps him for us to tell someone he is disabled and therefore requires a little more time for basic tasks. Yes, there are a few people it frightens, but most people are patient and understanding. Besides, it is good for people to learn that not everyone is normal. Normal sure is a funny word, isn't it? Who determines normalcy? What does it really mean? Maybe Joel is normal and we are not! Sorry to digress, but it is worth thinking about sometimes.

I do encourage parents to be honest with their children about abilities, limitations, weaknesses, and strengths, but to find a way to do so that is never abusive and only uplifting. This way, the child retains a strong sense of self-esteem while knowing his own challenges. Find the good; minimize the bad, but avoid the excessive use of impossible dreams that will not happen. Since the positive qualities of an autistic are unbounded, there is no need to dwell on the weaknesses. I believe that most autistic children and adults are well aware of the things they can't do well. It is one reason for the withdrawing of personality that often occurs.

Your job as a caregiver is to help him cope, to bring out his best, and to provide a sense of security in as little a restrictive environment as possible. All of this forms a young man who is comfortable in his skin, for the most part, and who knows he is loved by many. But how do we give him a sense of ambition and dreams without creating a false world? There is a balance that all parents work to achieve.

Forty-Three

Self-Reflection

My dad used to say, "Son, you take yourself too seriously. Enjoy life and laugh at yourself occasionally." I have learned to do so and try to avoid those introspective times of self-reflection and self-absorption. But, being a flawed human, I tend to operate in a vacuum of what is best for myself. This is not a great quality, but I have noticed that it is a trait common to everyone I meet. We tend to spend too much time in self-reflection. There is nothing wrong with this, unless our absorption excludes the rest of the world. My personal island is a myth, and to try to live on it, devoid of others, is both absurd and impossible. To take it another step further, excessive self-reflection is a burden and one that can shape your worldview, carrying your problems and mistakes everywhere you go. Yes, my dad was right; we do tend to take ourselves too seriously.

Now, let's talk about Joel and autism. As ironic as it seems, autistics do not generally spend much time in self-reflection. This seems a bold statement to make in light of the generally accepted attitude of autistics being withdrawn and into their own world. Yet being in your own world does not necessarily require self-absorption as much as it requires simply designing your own framework to fit your concept. Self-reflection is an exercise in creativity and imagination, both traits not common in autism. To self-reflect is to spend time learning about oneself and applying those truths in the outer world. As previously mentioned, too much self-reflection leads to self-absorption and, subsequently, to the removal of selfless altruism (All you Ayn Randians out there, don't get miffed yet!).

So, why do autistics remain quiet and seemingly caught up in themselves? What are they thinking about? In the case of Joel, each time I ask him to verbalize his thoughts, he tells me what he wants to do: eat, play the organ, go somewhere, or he tells me something he sees, touches, or is currently experiencing. But he has never told me some deep emotional thought that would be a kind of breakthrough as to what is in his head. I do suspect at times that he is ordering the world around him and trying desperately to make sense of it. But I do not believe that his quiet moments are due to any kind of self-reflection as much as due to his reorganizing that which confuses him.

But his confusion, his need for order, routine, organization, and planning, does not cause him depression or deep anguish; instead, it causes him immediate fright and insecurity. While emotions such as these would lead "normal" (that word again) people to examine themselves and their own deep-seated concerns, for an autistic, they are simply emotions of the moment and not worth great consternation over a period of time. It comes back to the difference between a life filled with imagination and a life filled with complexity. Imagination is a great gift and one that send us to worlds unknown and heights not attained by human beings, but imagination is the same thing that takes us to dark regions, fear, and suspicion. How often have we dreamed up a negative situation that didn't really exist? How often are we suspicious when there is no reason to be?

Self-reflection, to a point, can be gainful, causing us to learn more about ourselves, thereby resulting in greater productivity and general usefulness. Excessive self-reflection, however, can lead to self-absorption, taking us eventually to depression and anxiety. For

Joel, who is missing an imagination, these traits are non-existent. He is not burdened by any kind of extreme self-reflection and instead responds to life in two dimensions rather than three. This makes for a generally happy response to most situations, provided they make sense in his world. Maybe there is a magic to this idea, and maybe we can learn from this concept.

Forty-Four

Cause and Effect

Heading out on a Saturday morning to drop Joel off at his grandmother's house for the morning, I noticed on this slightly brisk day, which was guaranteed to warm up into the 80s in the afternoon, that Joel had donned a toboggan cap, a scarf, a heavy coat, and gloves. I gently, but also directly, told him that his clothes were too warm for the projected temperature of the day. As is typical for him, he disagreed and insisted on wearing those clothes.

Choosing not to argue at the moment, we climbed in the truck for the twenty-minute drive. I noticed that the temperature in the truck read 64 degrees and climbing. Mentioning this to Joel, I also said that it was likely going to be in the 80s by mid-morning with the sun shining brightly. He said that I was wrong and that it was going to snow.

Perplexed by this pronouncement, I asked him why he believed it would snow. His response was that he was dressed for snow . . . therefore . . . it would snow. I stayed quiet for a few minutes to reflect on this statement. Joel has never completely understood cause and effect. In some ways it has created some curiosity, but in other ways he simply rejects that idea. He knows that what he does can cause an effect of some kind or another, but he has a difficult time discerning or predicting what the effect will be. He cannot determine people's reactions, and he cannot determine his own place in creating certain responses in other people. It is all a mystery to him.

This is partly why he wears ties and suits to football games, why it seems okay for him to wander around or sit when others are standing, why he hugs when others are shaking hands, why he insists on playing the organ too loud, or the myriad of behaviors Joel tends to do. He does not see anything wrong and cannot assess how people will react to him. Not only that, but their reactions have little meaning to him. He resides in his own tinted existence, not worrying about how others see him. Consequently, he does not pass judgment on others' behavior other than those events learned specifically out of experience or a repetition of order. Cause and effect is peripheral at best in his world, a world without imagination and a world requiring routine and order.

Deep down, I suspect he knew that he could not cause it to snow simply by wearing warm clothes. He knows that neither he nor anyone else governs the snow or lack thereof. Yet because he gives no thought to the reactions of other people, and because he often confuses the cause and effect of his own behavior, he somehow converted his desire for snow into a kind of demand. His appearance, and yes, his preparation, ought to result in the weather change.

I convinced him to watch for the temperature to rise above 72 with the idea that a number would be the catalyst to change, and then I further convinced him to remove the toboggan cap, the gloves, the scarf, and, finally, the coat upon hitting 72. Reluctant at first, the rising temperature number was the final convincer, making Joel realize that his clothes did not cause the snow.

Still, what a nice dream for our dress to create weather change! Would it were so.

The tried and true parenting technique of the "strong" look will not work with autistics. Keep written instructions or suggestions on a card to show them.

Forty-Five

The Role as a Parent

If you are a parent of a child with special needs, one of the first things you need to do is to accept your role as a guardian, protector, guiding light, and the responsible entity of your child. Many parents expend great emotional energy trying to determine their own role as parents of a special-needs child. The first thing to establish is that you are the primary responsible person and will be as long as you live. This is not a choice; it is an obligation. It may be a burden, or it might be a blessing (or likely a mixture of both with emphasis on blessing), but it is the requirement for being the parent. Once you accept this as your duty, it makes other decisions much easier. You should not abdicate your responsibility to a school system, a set of teachers, or a government agency to find the secret for the happiness of your child. You are the expert, and you know what is best. You love the child more than anyone else, and you are responsible for providing for the child's physical needs as well as his emotional requirements.

Knowing this, however, does not necessarily mean that you are the sole caregiver throughout the rest of the child's life, but it does mean that you are overseer of the child and that you are the guardian. Your prime directive is to provide a safe, secure learning environment that allows your child comfort, happiness, and a purpose. In most cases, this is the home where the parents reside, but in some cases this is a special-needs residence.

185

Finding the right kind of special-needs home requires careful research, on-site evaluation, and money for the residence. Mostly, it requires that the person and the guardians be entirely comfortable with the setting.

Meanwhile, it seems to me that parents expend much time and energy both denying their child's situation and being afraid to accept any kind of responsibility for the child. In many ways, this is understandable due to the sheer amount of resources available to help and the amount of teachers involved in your child's education. The state (and this is true for most states) goes to great lengths to help ease the educational process and protect the child from failure in the classroom. Over a period of several years, it is easy for the parent to become somewhat complacent and even dependent upon the educational process to solve all the problems and turn out a product that is capable of contributing to society.

Unfortunately, while schools can help and all efforts are certainly worth it, in the end, the child still has limitations. The parent who denies the realities of the child's abilities, or lack thereof, is possibly a parent not providing for the welfare of the child and for the future. There is nothing to gain and much to lose by not being able to recognize the limitations of special-needs children. The parent should know that recognizing limitations does not mean using those challenges as excuses for mediocrity. Invoking high expectations on your child is the only way to promote the idea that there is a niche for all people.

But until the parent accepts the child as a special-needs child with disabilities, the child is actually endangered by a world that is not designed for those who have problems. So, in spite of the constant demands on the parents, it is an absolute mandate to provide a safe, secure, and comfortable world for your child, a world that allows him to reach his potential.

Chronicling the life of our autistic son Joel from his childhood to adulthood brings to mind the constant concern, the constant joy, and the emotional roller coaster that a special-needs child causes in a family. In the course of living our lives, we often encounter dramatic events that require our emotional reaction—events such as a loss, birthdays, tender moments, thrilling times, adventures, or an infinite amount of audacious and stunning things that happen to human beings. All these and more elicit great emotional responses from us. But once they are done, while vestiges of the experience remain, in general, the emotion reposes and we return to a calm ride on the sea.

Yet, having a special-needs child causes an entirely different set of emotions in a parent. Good parents will love, protect, and worry about their children all their lives. It is almost a mandated condition of parenting (and grandparenting, I hear) to spend a great deal of time being concerned about your children. For us, the same is true. We love our children, and each one is special, deserving our devoted love and attention forever. The difference is that the dramatic events that elicit great emotional responses turn away and go into repose. Parenting a child without disabilities provides opportunities for the human emotions to relax, to calm themselves, and to experience still waters after the turbulence.

Parenting a disabled child, however, can be likened to being on rough waters that will not change, will not become still, and will always threaten to overwhelm the boat. Furthermore, the boat remains on the water and will never come on land. Turbulence becomes a way of life on the open water, and any calm is relished but somehow anomalous in a quaking quagmire of constant contention. But wait, if all that is true and more, where is the pleasure, the joy, the blessings?

I recall hiking through the Franklin Mountains, as a teenager, while searching for and finding prickly pear cactus. After gathering the little pears, carefully, but thoroughly, we would cut out the tiny needles. It was painstaking work, due to the fear of needles getting stuck in our fingers or even in our tongues, but the joy from the taste of the jelly was worth the effort of preparing the pears for jelly. So it goes with raising a disabled child.

Unlike dramatic events that are dispelled, leaving behind vestiges of concern but ending in positive results, raising a disabled child has no end and requires an infinite amount of tenacity and patience. It is ubiquitous, difficult, and not for the faint of heart. A parent must apply due diligence to virtually everything, including hygiene, health, safety, education, and behavior. Somewhere in the transference from child to adult, the parents must find ways to make the child socially presentable, able to fit into the world, and able to contribute something to society.

I do believe that a parent of such a child must take some time for self-examination, because to learn about oneself is to be able to "learn" about others. A moment of selfishness or self-reflection can make one aware of a lifetime of selflessness. And selflessness is absolutely necessary for raising a disabled child to adulthood.

But like the prickly pear experience of my youth, the rewards are wonderful, and like the song says, "Love Changes Everything." To love your child is to do everything possible to help him or her regardless of the challenges in front. In some cases, love can take the form of institutional help or medical intervention, but, in most cases, love is the ruling factor in all decisions, for nobody knows your child the way you do.

Yet it is all difficult, and parents often question their own decisions along the journey. Are we indeed doing the right thing, the best thing, for our child? When Joel turned twenty-one, he gave a recital of nice Christmas music played on the organ to his friends, followed by a reception and a birthday cake for audience members. After Joel's recital, there were lots of smiles from people and congratulations were in order for Joel. As his parents, we were and are, of course, proud of our son, but we also remember the twenty-one years of challenges getting to this point. It hits home when the inevitable, well-intentioned person approaches us and says, "Joel is very lucky to have parents like you. You have obviously done a great job of raising him. He would not be where he is without you."

We receive these comments in kindness, with the grace and diffidence expected of our position. But it is with mixed emotions that we respond with, "Thank you." While, in many ways, it is true that Joel is fortunate to have two parents who care about his growth, his education, his progress, and his condition, in other ways, the comment reminds us of Joel's limits. We, as his parents, tend to see his potential, believing in what he can be and never letting go of the ideal. But what if we have been wrong? What if Joel really has very little potential?

Do other people see something that we do not see? Are we blinded by our love of our son to the point of not being able to act realistically in his best interests? Is Joel's success entirely dependent on our lifting him up? Does he walk on our feet . . . stand on our legs? Are we the escalator that emotionally and cognitively transports him from one place to another?

Maybe Joel's grandmothers played a significant role as well? Joel's teachers? Joel's friends? Obviously, assuming sole credit would be a selfish parental flaw, since raising him was a community effort in many ways.

One of the primary purposes of parenting is to encourage your children to be independent, to make their own choices, to live their own lives, and to become adults who are capable of navigating the turbulent waters of life. For an autistic, however, the capability is greatly limited. The rough waters require a lifeboat with an anchor, a solid protection base, and a constantly watchful eye out for the autistic child or adult.

The thing is this: we grow from adversity, and children find ways to be successful in the midst of their failures. When you skin your knee on the playground, you find ways to avoid doing so again while still enjoying the playground experience. For an autistic, the skinned knee happened without a direct cause. He will likely not learn from the event and may not be able to correct it the next time without some careful teaching. Once again, we find the idea of teaching independence to an autistic to be very difficult.

We have spent years working with our son to help him to be independent as much as possible, knowing that he will not be able to take care of himself in any kind of totally independent way (Of course, this brings to mind what independence even means, or if any of us are entirely independent, but that is another subject for the Libertarians of the world!). Are we to be thanked for our efforts? To be affirmed as good parents? Should we imagine that we have made a difference in Joel's life? Maybe so . . . but to me, it just seems like the work was our job as parents.

So, "Thank you," but maybe we didn't do well enough. Not sure . . . We have done the best we could. For the most part, I guess it has been pretty good.

As soon as a young child is diagnosed with Autism Spectrum Disorder, enroll him in speech therapy, physical therapy, and occupational therapy. The public schools may provide these services starting at age three.

Forty-Six

Isolation versus Collectivism

Parents with special-needs children often find themselves operating independently from the rest of the world in a need to stay isolated and emotionally protected. Experiences with those dramatic public instances of harsh judgment from others or embarrassing situations will make parents avoid such events and simply live in a type of cave of emotional hibernation from the rest of the world. It is just easier than going out in public.

But to remain in isolation is not to gain from the collective wisdom of other people, particularly family, friends, teachers, and those with training, knowledge, and sensitivity. Yes, the caregivers have the primary responsibility for the autistic child, but without the collective strength of many, the task of rearing the child can be insurmountable. Protection is essential; isolation is often necessary, but excluding those who can help in the process is to ignore the social responsibility required for the proper education of an autistic child.

Practicing a philosophy of congruence and independence allows a family to benefit from the support and resources that exist globally and locally. There are many who are willing to reach out and help in the process of raising the child, and there are a plethora of organizations designed to provide support in many different ways. Operating entirely congruently may be out of the question for many families with special-needs children, but living independently is not wise either.

In the healthy tension of isolation versus collectivism, the answer lies in the middle, with a balance and a trusting of instincts. Sometimes it is best for the child to be away from others, and sometimes it is best for the child to be with other people, learning proper behavior from adults and people who care.

Joel is now a contributing adult, because so many contributed to his growth. Grandparents, brothers, cousins, aunts and uncles, friends, teachers, and the loving attention of people who recognized a need has made all the difference in Joel's life.

Forty-Seven

Shopping With Joel

It's always an adventure of sorts when shopping with Joel. Needing some last-minute gifts, we headed to Bealls for one or two specific items. I tend to keep a running dialogue with Joel, most of which goes unanswered. But I like to talk with him and express my thoughts in the hopes that he will try to relate to my conversation, my feelings, and my goals. We spent a few minutes in Bealls, with Joel being very perplexed as to why the shirt we got for him for his birthday a few weeks earlier was the same one in the package at Bealls. I explained that they had several of the same color and type but reminded him that we were not there for him but instead were shopping for other people.

After leaving Bealls, we walked across the outdoor shopping center and stopped at Burke's Outlet. We walked to the men's section, and this time Joel began looking at the ties. It was more difficult this time to get him away, until I mentioned that we could wait until after Christmas and see if the ties were on sale. He liked that idea and we left. So far, he was not interested in buying something for any person other than himself!

Deciding to go to Walmart, we parked several miles away (okay, it felt like it anyway) and went inside. I reminded Joel several times to stay close, which was particularly important since he had forgotten his cell phone. I walked to the left to get some salmon for dinner, and when I turned around . . . Joel was gone. While looking for him and nearly panicking, I began to think logically about where he would go. *Gummy Worms—his favorite treat!* As I head toward that aisle, here he comes, holding two packages of Gummy Worms.

I reminded him to stay close to me, and we left Walmart (This was no easy task, since Joel stopped and talked to and hugged about five people on the way out.) and headed to J.C. Penney at the mall. We walked into Penney's, and Joel once again looked at the shirts and ties. Deciding to go next door to Hibbett Sports and hearing how thirsty he was, I asked him if he would like to go get a drink at Chick-fil-A. He said sure and left while I waited in a line to check out.

Soon, he returned holding a milk shake and a big smile on his face. The spoon was in it which was my first concern. He will not use a straw for any kind of ice cream drink. A spoon is always required. But as he stood there, I knew something else was wrong. Soon, he said, "Dad, once again we have to deal with the cherry."

Until I removed the cherry, Joel would not drink the shake. He would stand there holding it and staring at the cherry, and the drink would go untouched. So I took the cherry out and held it in my hand while checking out of the sports store. Joel said nothing more and waited for me on the bench outside of the store. I sat with him as he finished, and we returned to the truck for the trip home.

I was tired of Joel using my pants (We are close to the same size in pants in spite of his being taller and thinner.), and because of his insistence on wearing black, pleated pants, I finally convinced him that it was time to buy some new ones. Since we would soon be attending a band banquet, he did need some new clothes. Expanding this concept to getting him a complete suit, it was with great anticipation that we headed to J.C. Penney to buy new clothes, clothes that would hopefully prevent him from getting my clothes out of my closet!

On the way, it occurred to me to ask him some questions about work. He works every afternoon in the public library, putting away books that have been placed on the cart. Some days he puts away as many as seventy, while other days it is around thirty. The books range from fiction to reference to Children's books. He says he has NEVER placed a book in the wrong place, and he further insists that he knows the location of every book in the library. As we talked, I asked him if putting the books away required many steps. He said yes and said sometimes just 300 steps but other days as much as 700. A little surprised, although I probably should not be, I asked him if he counted his steps every day. He said yes.

More questioning revealed that he has counted his steps in various locations and various trips for ten years. There are about 350 steps from my office to the cafeteria, 450 from the library to the church, and 200 from church to my office. Having never given much thought to the number of steps from one place to another, I realized that for Joel, in many ways, every step is victory! Never easy for him, as he journeys, he is accomplishing something special and positive. Maybe we should all consider our steps along the way.

Back to the suit. Walking into J. C. Penney and heading for the men's section, Joel reminded me of the need to find pleated pants and a matching coat. This should have been a clue to the upcoming events. We proceeded to look at nearly every pair of black pants hanging or folded on the shelves. Identifying the pleated ones, we then could not seem to settle on the size. I kept mentioning that he probably was a 32/34, but he kept insisting that he was a 34/32. I did say that a waist size of 33 was probably about right, and he agreed. We found some black 33/34 that were perfect but couldn't find a matching coat. I found some 34/32 and a matching coat, but he was not happy. On and on it went, until finally I just said to buy whatever he wanted. This is a typical reaction to the frustration he presents.

In the end, he found a nice matching suit with pleated pants. We paid and went home where I collapsed on the couch. Of course, he was happy and got dressed in his new suit for the band banquet. While at the banquet, he spilled guacamole on his new coat which is currently at the cleaners!

Forty-Eight

Protection and Accommodation for Disabled Adults

W hen Joel was getting near the age of eighteen but still needed two more years of school before receiving his high school diploma, it occurred to me to ask what happens to him and countless others who have been guided, taught, and educationally nurtured throughout most of their lives. What do they do? Who helps them, and are we prepared as a society for an influx of adult-aged special learners?

I once read with interest, with a little shock, and with emotional disparity, an article about the American playwright, Arthur Miller, known for *Death of a Salesman*, and *The Crucible*. Unknown to most people, Arthur Miller had a Down syndrome son named Daniel. It is a dramatic story of a public figure (Arthur Miller was once married to Marilyn Monroe.) who rejected his son, sent him to an institution where he was mistreated, shuffled around, and finally adopted by a family he calls his own. Arthur Miller never checked on him, and only near the end of the playwright's life did he seek an opportunity to meet him. Ironically, in Miller's will, he made Daniel a rightful heir to his sizable fortune. The story of Arthur Miller and his son is also a historical, cultural study of the '60s, when parents did not know what should or could be done for their children with special problems.

A prominent well-known intellect, immensely respected for two long-running plays, in a moment of fear, or maybe anger, or lack of compassion, or maybe even misguided wisdom, sent his son to what he perhaps thought would be a better life for himself and the infant who was projected to have a shortened lifespan. Perhaps most dramatically, this is testimony to the strength, joys, challenges, and boundless optimism found in children with disabilities. Incidentally, it must be noted that after the birth of Daniel and his subsequent rejection, Arthur Miller did not produce any great works of consequence.

In some ways, society has grown out of the prejudice and confusion of how to deal with children who have learning disabilities and physical anomalies; at least we are more sympathetic and understanding of these children and have dedicated more education money to the learning process. With this emphasis has come a greater commitment on the part of parents to keep their children in the home, to avoid the institutions, and battle the learning challenges on several fronts. This idea comes at a good time in our culture with a stunning rise in children with autism and learning disabilities. Texas public schools are close to 12% in children enrolled in special education, and it is difficult to determine how many additional special-education children are enrolled in private education or various non-state-supported institutions.

So, with this knowledge, I come back to the question at hand: What will happen to these children when they become adults? Are these children, many of whom have great problems and many of whom have few, a drain on society without having enough redeeming qualities toward becoming contributing citizens? Or are there enough programs to help these children when they become adults, adults with job needs, transportation needs, food and clothing, and the need for independent living as much as possible. And, of course, there is the age-old question: Should the government even be involved in helping the disadvantaged? Private charity and family responsibility are the primary methods for reaching out to the adults in our community who are desperately in need, but somehow I suspect that many are not finding these sources. In the case of Daniel Miller, Arthur Miller's son, the state assumed responsibility but did an inadequate job at the time. Eventually, however, Daniel found a home and a loving family. How many out there are not as fortunate?

I believe there are indeed state-funded programs to help these adults, and I also want to believe that families are taking on more responsibility for their care. In our case, we have researched and sought legal counsel for ways to help Joel as he enters adulthood, and we have decided to take advantage of the Mental Health and Mental Retardation (MHMR) support system for helping Joel; plus, we have decided, after much thought and prayer, to assume responsibility for his care by keeping him with us at home until such a time that we are no longer able. There are still many questions we have regarding our son, such as a possible job, transportation, staying by himself, relationships, food, but, overall, we are confident in Joel's future.

Yet, I still wonder what kind of societal responsibility we have, what state resources are available, or how much family dedication there is for all those children not only with autism (Some are estimating the ratio of one out of every 165 children, or 1/165.), but also with other learning disabilities, who will, in the not so distant future, become adults. This is not a question merely for those of us with children who qualify but ultimately a question for everyone. At the same time, there is hope in this regard, for I was encouraged, in visiting with MHMR, to discover the diligent effort being made to identify adults in need of care. I look forward to this practice continuing.

I recall, with ironic and embarrassed amusement, the reactions of many people when handicapped parking places became the norm, when ramps for wheelchairs were being built, and when restrooms were given special stalls to accommodate the physically challenged. Some felt that we were catering to the needs of a small minority and rebuilding society to accommodate the very few with disabilities. The move toward a less-restrictive environment grew rapidly in the early 1970s with the U.S. Rehabilitation Act of 1973 that helped fund accessibility requirements, and the 1990 Americans with Disabilities Act (ADA) that increased awareness and physical requirements, and prevented job discrimination based on disabilities. ADA has also contributed to building code accessibility by insisting on entrance ramps, wider doors, seating capacity, restroom needs, lower water fountains, and required elevators. In addition, we have all experienced the abundance of handicap parking spaces (and perhaps emotion at those undeserving people who seem to take advantage of those spaces) which are intended to help disabled people have easier access to various facilities.

In some ways this has all been a drain on taxpayers, business owners, architects, and institutions. One could always attempt to make the old argument that the free market ought to determine the accommodations and needs of those who are disabled. Just as we tend to frequent the restaurant where we enjoy the food, the price, and the environment, so should a person with a disability frequent the businesses who provide the greatest accessibility for their needs. Those businesses who recognize those needs will build accordingly, with the result being increased profit margins. But in fact—is that true?

Without legislation, would there exist handicap parking spaces, or wider doors, or handicap bathroom stalls, or elevators in every building? I seriously doubt it. The market, correctly, caters to the needs of the majority and is governed primarily through the resulting demands of the people by a process known as 'supply and demand'. When there is a demand for particular goods, there is a supply developed to meet that demand, with an abundance of supply lowering the cost of the goods, and a limited supply causing greater demand and higher costs. But the question is: Would the people demand accommodations for those with disabilities and only frequent those establishments providing easy access? Maybe, but it is questionable, especially considering the small number of people with this serviceable requirement.

So now the government finds itself infringing on culture and society by seeking to legislate accessibility and services for those with disabilities. While it does not seem fair or right to force businesses and owners to provide easy access, and the cost can be astronomical in the end, it gives people with disabilities the freedom and right to shop, work, and live in our society that would otherwise be unavailable to them. This is an unusual and, perhaps, rare example of government intervention that demonstrates care, compassion, and positive results for disabled people.

But what does the future hold for those with mental disabilities, those whose inherent aptitude is limited, those without the ability to hold down a steady job, those who cannot drive, perhaps have trouble balancing a checkbook, or even have difficulty communicating? Do we treat them as pariahs, blights on society, as hopeless losers? In the not so distant past, we would have relegated them to prisons where many of them might have gotten worse and might never have known a free environment. Maybe we should quickly send them to institutions so as to avoid thinking about them. Or do we instead, as a civilized society, in an attempt to rise above the barbarisms of the past, provide options for them and find the ways and means to integrate them into society whenever possible? In other words, can we provide the least restrictive environment possible? Is there a place in our world for someone with a mental disability?

201

As we slowly but surely become a more civilized world, we may find ourselves in a difficult, but morally responsible, position to provide accommodations for the mentally handicapped as well as the physically handicapped. Obviously, every person is different, and some require greater care than others, and it could be a long haul requiring many years of contention, questions, and doubt, but I believe that we will one day embrace all those who have disabilities as deserving of their rightful place among the citizens of our world. Meanwhile, it becomes the responsibility and obligation for citizens to find ways to help their own and to continue to refine civilization to include those with disabilities. We have come a long way in this regard, and I anticipate future growth in awareness and accommodations.

Model patience to people in public places by allowing (requiring) the autistic person to answer for himself, order in a restaurant for himself, or pay for things himself, with as little help as possible.

After turning twenty-one, Joel needed an updated identification card, so we headed to the Department of Public Safety to get a new ID card. His card is carried around his neck with his house key. This helps him remember his home address and allows others to know him in case he is limited in his verbal expression on any given day. It is readily accessible, visible, and clearly delineates him as possibly needing help or protection. What better way to provide protection for our son than to ask the local law enforcement services to update his ID card for him.

We have struggled for years to achieve a balance of letting people know of Joel's disabilities but at the same time needing to allow him to fit in with society. It makes for a healthy tension in our presentation of our son. There have been countless times when I wanted to shout into a megaphone, "My son Joel is autistic and requires more time, patience, and understanding than most people." But how proper is it to label a human as different when there is also great gain in blending in with others? So we walk on the parental tightrope of helping him while encouraging a degree of independence. The ID around his neck is simply a tool to help him and others in case of a situation.

In the Department of Public Safety office, Joel and I approached the desk where I explained that he needed to update his ID card since he was now twenty-one. The lady at the desk shoved a form at us and said to answer questions one through eleven. I mentioned that he did not have or need a drivers license. She said that we had to fill it out anyway. Joel and I then walked over to the wall, stood at a counter, and began answering the questions on the form. No question was difficult, but they did require a moment of pause in answering. A funny moment occurred when the fourth question asked if Joel wanted to be an organ donor. He laughed at the question and said no, that he wanted to keep all his organs. I realized that he was thinking about pipe organs and not internal human organs. I explained to him about what it actually meant, and he decided that he would donate his organs.

The third question asked if he had any condition in communication that police officers would need to know. Joel said yes and wrote that he was verbally disabled—which is true. When we were nearly completed with the form, another rather brash lady approached Joel and proceeded to tell him that his current ID was invalid because it had a hole in it. We had punched a hole in his ID card to attach a lanyard to it and hang it around his neck. She was quite critical of this and told Joel that he was not to do that again. Joel had no clue about her criticism and simply nodded at her. I interrupted the harsh lady and asked her if she had a better method for Joel to use. We had a brief discussion about using a plastic holder and placing the ID inside it—easy enough solution.

We finished the form and returned to the first lady. She looked at Joel and said in a loud, rude voice, "Can you talk?" Joel nodded, and I began to seethe at her brusqueness. She then said louder, "Can you understand what I am saying to you?" As her voice got louder, my blood pressure rose several points. Joel looked at her quizzically and said that he understood her. She said that by answering yes to number three, we would need to fill out several more forms and get a doctor's statement. She said that it would be easier to say "NO", that he did not have a condition that prevented communication. I sighed and pointed out that his disability was well-documented at the Social Security Office as well as the County Courthouse. I then naively asked why the state law enforcement did not have access to the Social Security files or the county information. She told me, "We do not operate that way." I shrugged and said okay.

We then filled out the form again with number three as a "NO". She pointed out that Joel was not allowed to be an organ donor since he did not have a driver's license and then took the picture for the card. After finding out that the new ID card would arrive in approximately six weeks, we left. As we were leaving, the 2nd harsh lady sort of apologized for her rudeness and said that in the military they were not allowed to punch holes in anything. Since that made zero sense to me, and I'm sure Joel was completely in the dark on what the military had to do with anything, I simply nodded, said thanks, and we left.

It was not a good experience, and had Joel been by himself, it would have been a disaster. Our world is a difficult one for autistics. Forms, lines, terms, money, people, travel, and social behavior all make for a difficult existence for a disabled adult. Many of the things that are required are a mystery, and without our patience, kindness, and great tolerance, a disabled adult will not be able to function adequately. I would hope and encourage our "service" departments to take on a helpful approach to people and recognize that not everyone is the same. Rude behavior to a young man who cannot fully comprehend subtleties such as body language and inferred meanings, as well as needing to have extra response time, is unacceptable. In fact, rude behavior is unacceptable to anyone. Our son requires protection from the difficult challenges of the world. How sad it is when the challenge comes from the office workers of our law enforcement.

Tip:

When given the opportunity, explain to community or service workers that this person is autistic and needs extra response time when being asked questions. Asking another question or rephrasing the first when he has not answered quickly will just confuse him, and he may think you're asking a completely different question.

Forty-Nine

What do we do?

Good parents set out to love their children unconditionally and to remain dedicated to their success as contributing citizens, living a full and joyous life that is both independent but also socially congruent with family, friends, and professionals in the workplace. Parenting is not for the faint of heart and requires a constant blend of compassion, command, cooperation, forgiveness, trial and error, and non-stop love. If the quasi-comic statement is true that "there has never been a child raised properly," then all parents are flawed people simply doing the best they can to provide the kind of physical and emotional environment that allows for children to thrive, to achieve, and to be happy.

And such is the case for Joel. We have done our best to give him a sense of love and security, to provide for his needs, and to give him skills he needs to cope, to be successful, and to be as independent as possible. But he does have limitations that prevent certain kinds of professions and employment. His aptitude, his abilities, his responses, his perceptions, and his concepts of reality are not within the boundaries that we have established in our culture for great success. Joel is not well-designed to provide a good or service that is demanded in our growing and exciting economy. Functioning successfully as an independent adult is a difficult one for Joel as it is for anyone with a disability.

A broken toe will heal, a flat tire can be fixed, weak eyesight can be corrected, batteries for toys can be replaced, but autism is here to stay, at least for now. It is not correctible, nor can it be fixed. While autism is a challenge for parents, for educators, and for community members, it is the person with autism who suffers the most. But he does not suffer necessarily out of his own limitations but rather he suffers from a culture that is not designed for his disabilities. The autistic is generally happy with himself and not destined for a life of self-pity or serious depression. He spends little if any time on self-reflection and does not need to examine his own lack of particular skills in relation to other people.

As parents work diligently to find a way to help their children be safe and succeed, so also does society need to be reminded that there are many in our midst with disabilities who are deserving of an opportunity to be contributing citizens. Relegating them automatically to a life in an institution, while in some cases certainly necessary and beneficial, may, in some situations, be an example of giving up, of accepting a mediocre existence devoid of meaning. It is time to step forward and seek out ways to reach those with disabilities and specifically autism.

It is actually the same process as parenting but on a grander cultural scale. Trial and error, love and compassion, patience and experimentation can all lead to finding ways to help adults with disabilities develop meaningful and contributing lives. This likely will involve an efficient and economical public transportation system that allows those with disabilities to have freedom of location. It will also require identification of skills that match the individual with the abilities, skills that may or may not include visual abilities, organizational abilities, computer skills, error detection, ciphering, spelling, and the list continues. Once those identifications are made, it is time for careful training and much patience.

Employers should work to find an environment that is free from distractions, quiet, ordered, and has a visual component to the task. Once the environment is conducive to helping autistics succeed, the training can begin. In many ways, just like parenting or teaching, the wrong kind of trainer will likely result in failure of the process. Yet a good trainer with knowledge and understanding of the disability can provide tools the autistic needs for achievement. This kind of commitment gives autistics a "running start" toward success. Granted that an employer cannot sacrifice great time and lost production to the process, in the end, in most cases, the gain is greater than the loss.

Perhaps there will be a day, and I suspect this is already occurring in many locations, where strategic identification of skills in adults with disabilities can lead to specific employment and result in disabled workers well-suited for certain jobs. Unfortunately there is no one mold that fits all, but with patience and flexibility, many adults with autism and other disabilities can find meaningful and practical application for their skills. While it took many years, we were able to identify a skill in Joel that allowed him to be successful.

We are far from perfect or even ideal parents, and the mistakes we have made could fill up another book. But our constant efforts and our willingness to try different approaches has led to some degree of success. When you go fishing and realize that something is not working, you change baits or lures hoping that you will find the one that will work. Such is parenting an autistic child. Not everything works, and sometimes nothing seems to work, but giving up is not an option. What works one day may or may not work the next. The magic bullet does not exist, and the secret formula is no real secret. The formula is comprised of effort and creativity, and mostly filled with nonstop love.

There is a plethora of resources available to help parents and caregivers deal with autism. Nearly countless websites, books, organizations, and a myriad of conferences exist to help autistics and those involved in their upbringing. In addition, new research, suggestions for treatment, and methods for education are abundant and active, bringing a social awareness and consciousness not only to educators but to people in the workforce as well. All these and more are generating great sensitivity and interest in autism and how to help those with this disability. It is an exciting and energetic time, and there is no lack of information to help deal with autism and with learning disabilities in general.

For parents seeking help, it is there. For educators of autistic children, help is present. For a society dealing with what seems to be the growth, or at least the identification, of those with autism or Autism Spectrum Disorders, there are many organizations eager to help. And yet, in spite of all the information, the resources, and the help, autism remains a difficult and mysterious disability and one that seems to have no easy answer. The pain, the sorrow, and the almost non-stop challenges associated with autism are, at times, balanced with the joys and the innocence that often accompany the disorder.

There is a productive place in our workforce and in our world for those with autism, but only if employers are willing to take a risk and willing to find a niche for adults with the disability. It will require tremendous patience and a broad societal love to learn to accept these adults, and it will require a level of understanding and trial and error to make them productive in a world that is not necessarily conducive for autistics. But the gain is worth the challenge, as we seek to help autistic adults become contributing members of society. We must all remember that the world is a strange place to an autistic. Perhaps it is time to make it a comfortable and meaningful existence for those who see the world through different lenses. It is a big world, and there is a place in it for everyone.

Final dialog

Driving our twenty-five minute commute from school to home, Jacob, the oldest, was in the front seat of the Suburban. Joel, the middle one, in 3rd grade, was in the backseat, and Jordan, in first grade, was in the "very back", as they called it.

Mom: Jacob, do you have homework?

Jacob: Yes, a little bit. I finished most of it at school in class.

Mom: Okay, good. Jordan—homework?

Jordan: I have to read my library book.

(Already having looked in Joel's backpack before leaving school to make sure he had his assignment folder, she checked to see what homework he had and made sure he had the correct textbooks—Mom already knows what homework he has.)

Mom: Joel, you have math and social studies homework. We'll do it as soon as we get home.

Joel: I want to ride my bike first.

Mom: Nope—homework first, then bike riding.

Joel: No! Bike first, then homework.

Mom: (sigh) Joel, let's do homework first and get it out of the way so it's not hanging over your head. Then you can ride your bike. (Thinking, *If we have time.*)

Silence for several minutes . . .

Joel: Mom, you mean like a crown?

Mom: Like a crown . . . what?

Joel: My homework—does it hang over my head like a crown?

Mom: (amazed, but a little saddened, thinks, *When will I learn not to use figures of speech with my literal, autistic, never a dull moment son??*)

(Jacob and Jordan, smiling at their amazing brother, listen as their mom once again tries to get into Joel's world and explain what it is she really means . . .)

About the Author

Robert L. Tucker is the Dean of Music, Fine Arts, and Extended Education at Howard Payne University in Brownwood, Texas. A musician with skills and experience at horn playing, composition, conducting, arranging, and church music, Dr. Tucker enjoys exercising, reading, blogging, speaking, and drinking a good cup of coffee. He and his wife Clairissa are the parents of three children, Jacob, Joel, and Jordan, and are available for workshops and presentations on Autism Spectrum Disorders.